THE RUSSIAN LANGUAGE
A BRIEF HISTORY

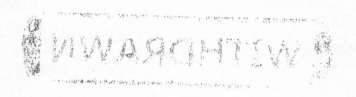

THE
RUSSIAN LANGUAGE
A BRIEF HISTORY

G. O. VINOKUR

Translated by MARY A. FORSYTH
Edited by JAMES FORSYTH

CAMBRIDGE
AT THE UNIVERSITY PRESS
1971

Published by the Syndics of the Cambridge University Press
Bentley House, 200 Euston Road, London N.W.1
American Branch: 32 East 57th Street, New York, N.Y.10022

© this translation Cambridge University Press 1971

Library of Congress Catalogue Card Number: 70–127238

ISBN: 0 521 07944 6

Printed in Great Britain
at the University Printing House, Cambridge
(Brooke Crutchley, University Printer)

PREFACE

G. O. Vinokur's Русский язык—исторический очерк remains unique among histories of the Russian language in combining an outline of the detailed facts of historical phonology and morphology with an overall view of the development of the language as a social phenomenon and means of literary expression. It is these qualities which make it eminently worth translating into English so many years after its first publication in 1943, as a readable introduction to the history of Russian.

Professor Grigoriy Osipovich Vinokur was born in 1896 in Warsaw. He was educated in Moscow and, apart from two years as an interpreter in Estonia and Latvia in 1920–2, spent the whole of his distinguished career there. From 1933 he worked in the Academy of Sciences of the USSR on the Academy edition of Pushkin's works, and on Словарь языка Пушкина. He died in 1947.

The present edition is a translation of the text published in 1959 in the volume of Vinokur's Избранные работы по русскому языку edited by S. G. Barkhudarov. An introductory note to that edition states:

This work was published in 1943. In the Preface to it G. O. Vinokur wrote that the book 'was written neither for specialists nor for self-instruction, and without any scholarly or pedagogical pretensions. For this reason it does not have the normal apparatus of a learned work, and does not contain lengthy arguments or complicated demonstrations of theories. It is meant simply as a book for reading, containing a specialist's account of what is bound to be of interest to anyone concerned not only with Russia's past but also with its language.' The author went on to say: 'The type of exposition adopted has prevented me from undertaking in this little book any strictly linguistic analysis. Instead of this I demonstrate the state of the Russian language at various stages of its history by the quotation of extracts from texts of various dates and types. In the quotations from the earlier texts the orthography has been simplified. From the 19th century onwards texts are given in modern orthography.'

In the present edition [1959] *The Russian Language* is published with certain omissions, chiefly in chapter 1. Chapter 12 has also been omitted.

These omissions have not been restored in this translation, since they represent on the one hand a few dubious references to a pre-Indo-European substratum, inserted in lip-service to the then prevailing 'New linguistic doctrine' of N. Ya. Marr,[1] and on the other

[1] Cf. Murra, J. V. and others, *The Soviet Linguistic Controversy*, New York, 1951.

an epilogue on 'The Russian Language and Patriotism' inspired by the Second World War, which adds nothing to the main theme of the book. Some further omissions of a political nature have been made, and these are indicated by dots. Explanations added to the text by the editor are enclosed in square brackets.

English translations have been given for the earlier and more difficult quotations, and some maps and footnotes added. As far as possible stress marks have been supplied for all Russian words and texts, since only with their help can the reader gain some idea of the sound of Old Russian.

The book was originally dedicated by Vinokur to his teacher the distinguished lexicographer D. N. Ushakov.

J.F.
Aberdeen, 1970   M.A.F.

CONTENTS

List of maps and illustrations   *page* ix

Symbols used   x

 1 The Slavonic languages   1

 2 Russian dialects   10

 3 The origin of the Russian literary language   21

 4 Texts in the history of Russian   30

 5 The structure of Old Russian   41

 6 The Russian literary language in the earliest period   52

 7 The literary language in the 15th–17th centuries   68

 8 Towards a single Russian language   82

 9 The literary language of the Age of Classicism   97

10 The creation of the national standard language   108

11 The literary language in the 19th and 20th centuries   126

Further Reading   139

Index   143

MAPS AND ILLUSTRATIONS

The Slavonic languages in the 20th century (*Map*)   *page* 2

Russian dialects (*Map*)   11

Probable approximate location of the East Slavonic
   tribes in the 9th century A.D. (*Map*)   17

Glagolitic and Cyrillic uncial scripts   25

Medieval Russia (*Map*)   31

16th-century half-uncial and 17th-century cursive scripts   33

SYMBOLS USED

Most of these are explained where they occur, but the following are of wider occurrence.

International Phonetic Alphabet (I.P.A.) symbols:

ḍ, ṣ, ḷ, etc. indicate palatalised consonants
ɣ   like English *h* but pronounced with voice
e   the vowel in French 'thé'
ɛ   the vowel in English 'met'
ə   the 'neutral' vowel in the second syllable of English 'over'
i   the vowel in English 'free'
ɪ   unstressed i
j   like *y* in English 'yes'
u   the vowel in English 'shoe'
'   indicates that the following syllable is stressed

Words in I.P.A. transcription are enclosed in square brackets.

Other symbols:

ǫ is like the vowel in French 'dans' (I.P.A. ã)
ę is like the vowel in French 'vin' (I.P.A. æ̃)
′ indicates that the preceding consonant is palatalised
> 'becomes'
< 'is derived from'

Some obsolete letters occur in the texts. Their names and modern equivalents are as follows:

ѣ (ять)	е
і (десятери́чное и)	и
ѵ (и́жица)	и
ѕ (зело́)	з
ѳ (фи́та)	ф

1

THE SLAVONIC LANGUAGES

Russian is a member of the large group of Slavonic languages, spoken by about three hundred million people in all, a little less than half of whom use Russian. On the basis of the similarities existing between them, the Slavonic languages can be divided into three groups: the western, southern and eastern. To the western Slavonic languages belong Czech, Slovak, Lusatian[1] (Upper Lusatian in Saxony, Lower in Prussia), Polish, Kashubian (in Polish Pomerania), and the language of the Polabian Slavs, who became Germanised towards the end of the 17th century, but whose language is preserved in a few documents. To the southern Slavonic languages belong Bulgarian, Serbo-Croatian and Slovene. To the eastern—Russian, Ukrainian and Belorussian.

Despite the numerous differences which exist between the groups of Slavonic languages and between individual languages within these groups, their grammatical structure and vocabulary show such a close affinity that the only possible explanation is that they originated from a common source. The historical evidence leads us to conclude that at the beginning of our era the Slavonic languages still possessed a considerable unity. Information about them which can be considered reliable dates only from the 6th century A.D. The historical sources of this period already mention three groups of Slavonic tribes and hence [presumably] of languages. But even in the 9th and 10th centuries, at the time when the first writings in Slavonic were making their appearance, the Slavonic languages still retained so many features in common, especially in grammatical structure, that the separate groups were able to use one common written language. This was Old Slavonic or Old Church Slavonic, about which more detailed mention will be made later.

The Slavonic languages constitute one of the largest members of the Indo-European group. In addition to the Slavonic languages this

---

[1] Also known as Wendish or Sorbian. [Ed.]

1

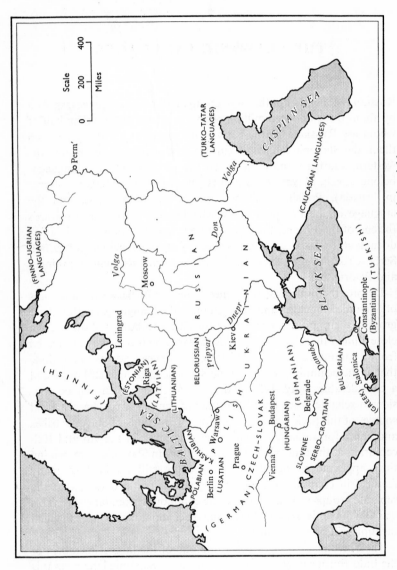

The Slavonic languages in the 20th century and their neighbours

The Slavonic languages

family includes Greek, Latin (with the modern Romance languages: French, Italian, Spanish, Rumanian, etc.), Germanic (English, German, Dutch, Swedish, etc.), Celtic (Irish, Gaelic, Breton, etc.), Baltic (Lithuanian, Latvian), Albanian, Armenian, several languages of India (with the ancient literary language Sanskrit), ancient and modern languages of Persia, and the dead languages Hittite and Tokharian[1] which came to light relatively recently.

Just as the Slavonic languages exhibit interrelationship, so each of the members of the Indo-European group of languages represents a particular development and modification of a common linguistic system, the features of which become apparent through a comparative-historical study. Such modern languages as English and Albanian, Persian and Yiddish [the dialect of German used by eastern European Jews], Irish and Russian have almost nothing in common. Nevertheless the history of these languages proves beyond all question that each one is simply a new and independent continuation of the same basic linguistic stock transformed to the point of un-recognisability. Just as all the Slavonic languages have as their source one language, Common Slavonic, so all the Indo-European languages go back to one language, Common Indo-European.

Of course none of these parent languages is known to us as an entity, and they never can be known. We possess no texts written in them, and we can get an impression of their structure and composition only by means of the comparative-historical study of those languages which have come down to us in documents or which continue to be used at the present day. But since the most ancient forms of the various Indo-European languages available to us are at different stages in their historical development, it is difficult to collate chronologically the separate conclusions which emerge from the comparative study of various features of their structure and composition. Therefore all we have to work on are isolated and disconnected traces of a certain linguistic system—a system which we are unable to reconstruct in its entirety. Moreover, it is improbable that this system ever included at any given time all those features which philologists have discovered, so that we are not justified in considering it as a concrete cultural and historical phenomenon. The expression 'parent language' was formerly understood by the

---

[1] Recorded respectively in 2000–1000 B.C. in eastern Asia Minor, and in the 7th–6th centuries B.C. in Central Asia. [Ed.]

Romantics in its literal sense. Considering it as a real language with a self-contained and complete structure, they even tried to compose connected literary texts in the reconstructed parent language. But in modern linguistics this expression is no more than a term with a conventional meaning, namely, a certain stock of regular correspondences established after a comparative-historical study of a group of languages, expressed in convenient formulae. Thus, for instance, the expression 'the Indo-European dorsal consonant k' is a formula covering the correspondence of Latin and Greek k, German h, Slavonic and Iranian s, Lithuanian $\check{s}$, Sanskrit ς,[1] as for example in the words for 'hundred'—Greek 'hekaton', Latin 'centum' (originally in Latin c stood for the sound k), German 'hundert', Russian 'sto' (сто), Old Iranian 'satəm', Lithuanian 'šimtas', Sanskrit 'çatam'. All these are undoubtedly one and the same word which has acquired different forms in the various languages at various periods, and the phonetic correspondence between these different forms is regular—that is, it repeats itself in other cases, e.g. in the words for 'ten'—Greek 'deka', Latin 'decem', German 'zehn' (from the earlier 'zehan'), Russian 'd′es′at′' (десять), Old Iranian 'dasa', Lithuanian 'dešimtas', Sanskrit 'daça', etc. But exactly how the words meaning 'hundred' or 'ten' *sounded* in the Indo-European parent language cannot be established with any exactitude. Moreover, even if this were possible, it would still be impossible to decide whether the 'original' reconstructed form of a given word could be correlated chronologically with the 'original' forms established for other words.

Nevertheless, it remains proved beyond any shadow of doubt that the Indo-European languages are genetically related in groups, and among each other within these groups... The Slavonic languages are typical Indo-European languages...

However, the Slavonic languages possess some features exclusively their own, which distinguish them as a whole from other Indo-European languages. Two phenomena in the field of speech sounds are particularly relevant. These are: firstly, the consistent and systematic opposition between the front and back vowels,[2] that is to say the vowels 'softening' or not 'softening' the preceding consonant; secondly, the elimination of originally closed syllables—that is

---

[1] The last two represent English *sh* and German *ch* in 'ich', respectively. [Ed.]
[2] Typical front vowels in Russian are those represented by the letters и and e, back vowels by o, y and ы. [Ed.]

4

syllables ending in a consonant—and the subsequent development of new closed syllables on a different basis.

The opposition of front and back vowels has had a particularly marked effect on the fate of the velar[1] consonants г, к and х. On two occasions in the prehistoric period these consonants underwent a change wherever they occurred before front vowels. This happened in all the Slavonic languages. In the first place every г, к or х preceding a vowel of the type *e* or *i* changed respectively to the palatal fricative ж, ч or ш.[2] (All three of these were originally pronounced soft, but in Russian ж and ш became hard at a considerably later date.) This change explains the alternation of consonants г/ж, к/ч, х/ш in modern Russian in such cases as Бог—Бо́же, пеку́—пече́нье, мох—мши́стый, etc. Later, but still before the appearance of written texts, those same consonants г, к and х where they occurred before front vowels arising from a new source (from the Indo-European diphthong *oi*) changed respectively to the sibilants з, ц and с.[3] This explains the alternation of consonants characteristic of Old Russian: г/з, к/ц, х/с, as for example in нога́—dat. and prep. нозѣ́[4] 'leg', рука́—dat. and prep. руцѣ́ 'hand', грѣхъ—plural грѣси́ 'sin'. These mutations disappeared in Russian at a later period. Compare also the modern Russian word цена́ 'price', which corresponds to the Lithuanian word 'kaina' having the same meaning. An important consequence of the opposition of the two types of vowels has been to preserve the distinction between the hard and soft consonants, as, for example, in the words дань—день, волка—вилка, etc., which have been preserved in Russian and Polish, and which are so difficult for speakers of the Germanic and Romance languages.

The elimination of the primordial closed syllables had the effect that originally in all the Slavonic languages a syllable could end only in a vowel sound, and therefore that no word could end in a consonant. In the modern Slavonic languages this is not the case. But two features of the Slavonic languages are relics of the former absence of closed syllables, viz.: the comparative rarity of clusters of consonants, and the fact that the lowest level of articulatory force between

[1] So called because their point of articulation—where the passage of air through the mouth is obstructed by the tongue to produce the sound—is the velum or soft palate near the back of the mouth. [Ed.]

[2] This is known as the 'first palatalisation'. [Ed.]

[3] This is known as the 'second palatalisation'. [Ed.]

[4] The letter ѣ is discussed on pp. 12, 41.

neighbouring syllables within a word [i.e. the syllable boundary, Ed.] generally occurs after a vowel, for example ce-стра, вну-три, and not сес-тра, внут-ри etc. This 'law of open syllables', as it is called, explains many of the peculiar correspondences, mentioned below, between Slavonic and the other Indo-European languages, as well as among the Slavonic languages themselves.

In the province of grammar the Slavonic languages have preserved many features which the other Indo-European languages have lost. Almost all the Slavonic languages (with the exception of Bulgarian) have preserved the ancient system of declension of nouns, adjectives and pronouns. Of the original eight Indo-European cases the Slavonic languages have lost only one, the ablative, the functions of which were transferred to the genitive. In modern Russian there is also no vocative case, but this was a comparatively recent loss, the majority of Slavonic languages having preserved it to the present day. On the other hand, the dual number,[1] well represented in early Slavonic texts, is now known only in Kashubian and Lusatian, even there, however, being in a state of atrophy. An original feature found in most Slavonic languages is the development in declensions of the category of 'person or not person', or 'animate' and 'inanimate', expressed formally by the replacement in certain conditions [most obviously in referring to living beings of male sex] of the original form of the accusative case by a form identical with the genitive, e.g. купи́ть вола́ 'to buy an ox' instead of the old купи́ть волъ.

Another feature, common to the Slavonic and Baltic languages, is the development of a class of compound adjectives (добрый, добрая, доброе) by the addition to the original substantival adjective forms (добръ, добра, добро) of a pronominal element (и, я, e 'he, she, it'). These parallel forms of adjectives have served as the basis for a characteristic differentiation in their syntactical use, as a result of which in modern literary Russian the 'short' form is used only in the role of predicate, and the compound form as either predicate or attribute (compare on the one hand отéц добр, and on the other до́брый отéц and отéц до́брый). In the majority of modern Slavonic languages the old substantival forms of adjectives have already died out or are in process of doing so.

---

[1] A set of forms distinct from the singular on the one hand and the plural (three or more) on the other, expressing the 'twoness' of the thing concerned, e.g. the pronouns вѣ 'we two', ва 'you two', etc. [Ed.]

The Slavonic languages

There have been many new developments also in the verb forms of the Slavonic languages, not only in various tense forms, but also and in particular in the formation of pairs of verbal stems expressing aspect by means of prefixes and suffixes (писать—подписать—подписывать, забыть—забывать, etc.). From the point of view of syntax we must mention the use of the genitive case instead of the accusative in negative statements (найти книгу 'to find a book'—не найти книги 'not to find a book'), the development of the 'predicative instrumental' (быть студентом 'to be a student'), and the absence of present tense forms of the copula 'to be' (он был студент 'he was a student'—он студент 'he is a student').

Finally, in their vocabulary the Slavonic languages have certain distinctive features which set them apart from the other members of the Indo-European family... The basic groups of ancient cultural terms on the whole represent the common Indo-European stock; for example, the names of the most important degrees of family relationship: мать 'mother', дочь 'daughter', сестра 'sister', сноха 'son's wife' [cf. German 'Schnur'], деверь 'husband's brother' [cf. Greek 'daēr', German 'Schwager'], etc.; various technical processes, e.g. писать 'write' [originally 'trace', 'paint', cf. Latin 'pingo'], тесать 'hew smooth' [cf. Greek 'tektōn'—'carpenter'], шить 'sew', вить 'twine, wind' [cf. Latin 'vieo'], печь 'bake'; certain domestic animals, e.g. кот 'cat', овца 'sheep' [cf. 'ewe', Latin 'ovis'], свинья 'pig' [cf. 'swine']; dwellings and settlements, e.g. дом 'house' [cf. Latin 'domus'], двор 'courtyard, homestead' [cf. 'door'], etc. However, there are also certain specifically Slavonic words, the origin of which is less clear. For instance, none of the Slavonic languages possesses the Indo-European names for 'horse' or 'dog', and the general Slavonic words for these—конь (or комонь) and пес—have no Indo-European cognates. (Russian, it should be noted, has names for these animals which no other Slavonic language has—лошадь and собака: these were borrowed at a much later date from the east.) Other specifically Slavonic words include вол 'ox', поле 'field', племя 'tribe', староста 'elected headman, foreman' and many others.

These then are, in outline, the peculiarities which belong to the Slavonic languages viewed as a whole. But by the time of the appearance of written Slavonic texts in the second half of the 9th century, noticeable differences already existed between the Slavonic languages. There is no doubt that Russian by this time already possessed certain

7

f the most important features which distinguish it from the other Slavonic languages. These specific traits of Russian which arose in the prehistoric period are most easily demonstrated in the realm of phonetics. The basic characteristics are as follows.

(1) In Russian the original combinations *tj*, *dj*, were replaced, in contrast to the other Slavonic languages, by the sounds ч and ж respectively. Instead of *tj*, *dj* we find in Polish *c* [cf. English *ts*] and *dz*; in Czech *c* [cf. English *ts*] and *z*; in Serbian ħ [cf. English *t* in 'tune', approaching *ch* in 'church'] and ђ [cf. English *d* in 'dew', approaching *j* in 'June']; in Bulgarian щ [cf. English *sht*] and жд. For example the Russian свечá 'candle' (cf. светúть) and сáжа 'soot' (cf. сад-ить) correspond to Polish 'świeca', 'sadza'; Czech 'svíce', 'saze'; Serbian 'свећа', 'caђa'; and Bulgarian 'свещ', 'сажда'. In the same way as *tj*, the combination *kt* changed before the front vowels, e.g. Russian печь 'bake' (from пек-ти—cf. first person singular пекý), Polish 'piec', Serbian 'пећи', etc.

(2) The combinations consisting of a vowel and a liquid consonant between two consonants, which can be represented by the formulae *tort*, *tolt*, *tert*, *telt* (where *t* stands for any consonant) are replaced in Russian by the combinations *torot*, *tolot*, *teret*, because of the tendency towards open syllables mentioned earlier. This is called полноглáсие [or 'pleophony']. In the other Slavonic languages the closed syllable was disposed of in a different way. In Bulgarian, Serbian and Czech we find *trat*, *tlat*, *tret*, *tlet* (with a long *e*), in Polish *trot*, *tlot*, *tret*, *tlet* and so on. Thus, for example, corresponding to the Lithuanian 'gardas'—'sheep-pen', 'hurdle' [cf. English 'garden', Ed.], we have Russian гóрод, Bulgarian and Serbian 'град', Czech 'hrad' and Polish 'gród'; corresponding to the Lithuanian 'galva', we have Russian головá, Bulgarian and Serbian 'глава', Czech 'hlava', Polish 'głowa',[1] and so on.

(3) Apparently, not long before the appearance of the first written Slavonic texts the Russian language lost the nasal vowels ǫ and ę,[2] which had existed at one time in all the Slavonic languages, and are now preserved only in Polish and in some Macedonian dialects. In Russian, instead of the nasal ǫ we find *u*, and instead of the nasal ę—*a* preceded by a soft consonant or *j* (this is represented by the letter я). Thus the Russian зуб corresponds to the Polish 'ząb' (the

---

[1] The pronunciation of Polish ł is similar to English *w*. [Ed.]
[2] In Old Slavonic texts these are written ѫ and ѧ respectively. [Ed.]

The Slavonic languages

Polish letter *ą* represents the nasal *ǫ*), the Russian пять to the Polish 'pięć', etc.

The three significant features mentioned above, together with other less important ones, hold good also for Ukrainian and Belorussian. In other words—these are general East Slavonic features which had arisen in all the spoken dialects of the East Slavs before the time of the appearance of the first written texts.

What place do the East Slavonic languages occupy as a whole in relation to the two other Slavonic language groups? On the whole the East Slavonic languages are genetically nearer to the South Slavonic languages than to West Slavonic. This opinion is founded mainly on two phenomena which had developed in the pre-literary period in both the East and South Slav groups, but which were unknown in the Western group. Firstly, in East and South Slavonic the consonants г and к underwent the Second Palatalisation—changing to з and ц respectively—because of a following front vowel [originally written ѣ, Ed.], even where they were separated from this vowel by the consonant в, e.g. Russian звезда́ 'star', Serbian 'звезда', but Polish 'gwiazda', Czech 'hvězda'; similarly Russian and Serbian цвет 'flower', but Polish 'kwiat', Czech 'květ'. Secondly, the original consonant groups *tl, dl*, which were preserved in the west, were simplified in the south and east to *l*, e.g. Russian плету́—плела́ (from плетла) 'plaited', веду́—вела́ (from ведла) 'led', and Serbian 'плела, вела', but Polish 'pliotła', 'wiodła'. On the other hand there are certain points which the east and west have in common to the exclusion of the south—points which we can contrast with the features which unite the south and east. The most important of these is the change in West and East Slavonic of the original combinations *or, ol* before consonants at the beginning of a word to *ra, la* under certain conditions, and to *ro, lo* under others, while in the south in place of these combinations we find only *ra, la*. Compare, for example, Russian ло́коть 'elbow' and Polish 'łokieć', but Serbian 'лакат'; Russian ро́вный 'even', Polish 'równy', but Serbian 'равни' (Russian ра́вный is a Church Slavonicism). Thus in some instances the language of the eastern Slavs has affinities with the southern Slavonic languages and in other instances with the western; but on the whole the internal genetic relations between the different groups of Slavonic languages are so complex that they defy attempts to set them out in a simple comprehensive scheme.

9

2

RUSSIAN DIALECTS

The term 'Russian language' is used to describe, on the one hand, the Russian literary language, and on the other, the totality of the numerous local dialects spoken in Russia. By the term 'Russian literary language' we generally understand the national language, the language of Russian culture—that is, the language of the state, of scholarship, of the press, and so on. Its most typical models are contained in literature in the widest sense of the word—письменность[1]—but to a considerable extent the everyday speech of the educated stratum of society, the intelligentsia, coincides with the literary language.

Local town dialects show the interaction, in one way or another, between the general literary language and the local rural dialects. The latter can be classified into various groups in accordance with the similarities and differences existing between them. Three wide groupings of Russian dialects are generally recognised: northern, central and southern.

The northern group includes the dialects of Novgorod, Olonets, Archangel (the dialects of the White Sea coast—Поморье), Vologda, Vyatka, the upper and middle Volga, the Urals, and many Siberian dialects. In the sphere of pronunciation the following two features are characteristic of all north Russian dialects.

Firstly, as a general rule, in the north the quality of a vowel does not depend on whether it is stressed or unstressed, or at least does so to a much lesser extent than in the south. This characteristic of northern pronunciation is called оканье, since *o* and *a* are differentiated in an unstressed position (o is pronounced everywhere as *o*) e.g. трава́ [tra'va] but вода́ [vo'da].

Secondly, in northern pronunciation the quality of a vowel depends to a very great extent on the consonants on either side of it—their hardness or softness. Thus, in many northern dialects *a* after a soft

---
[1] See the note on this word on p. 21. [Ed.]

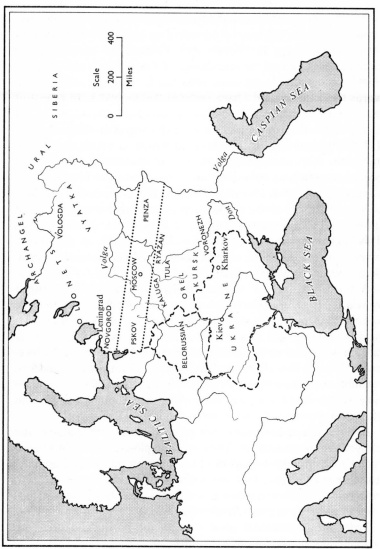

Russian dialects. (∙∙∙ Approximate boundaries of middle Russian dialect group)

consonant, and especially between two soft consonants, is replaced by *e*, so that they pronounce зять 'son-in-law', опять 'again' and мячик 'ball' as зеть, опеть, мечик, while грязь 'dirt' and пять 'five' are pronounced грезь and петь respectively, but the adjectives from them are nevertheless pronounced as грязный and пятый. In many dialects, e.g. in Olonets and Vologda, in exactly similar circumstances we find the interchange of *e* and *i*, e.g. хлеб—хлибец 'loaf', сено 'straw'—на сине, вера 'faith'—к вире, etc. In such words the sounds *e* and *i* have replaced the original ѣ. In general it must be noted that in the majority of northern dialects, in contrast to the south, the vowels ѣ and e have developed in different ways. Till the present day in the north, in words in which ѣ formerly appeared, such as сѣно and лѣто, a characteristic closed vowel occurs, intermediate between *e* and *i*, not unlike the French closed vowel *é* [ˈşeno, ˈļeto]. This sound is heard, for instance, in the dialects of Vyatka and the White Sea area. In certain other places instead of the original ѣ an *i*-type vowel occurs in all positions: [ˈşino, na ˈşiɲe]. This is characteristic of the Novgorod group. Only in a restricted number of cases, for example in certain dialects along the Volga, does *e* occur regularly in place of ѣ—[ˈşɛno, ˈļɛto].

A further feature of northern dialects is that *yod* [j] between vowels tends to disappear, with the consequent fusion of the two vowels. Thus instead of знает [ˈznajɪt] they say знаэт or even знат, with the *a* prolonged to a greater or lesser degree [znaːt]. Similarly работаэм or работам, Сысоэв or Сысов [adjective from the forename Сысой]. This elision explains adjective forms which appear to resemble the old nominal or 'short' forms, but in fact are contractions of the long forms, e.g. нова изба, така хороша книга, село Ильинско [instead of новая, такая хорошая, Ильинское].

In the realm of consonants two general features are characteristic of northern pronunciation. The first is the plosive г [cf. *g* in English 'good'], which coincides with the literary pronunciation, and secondly цоканье and чоканье. This means that ц and ч are not distinguished, both being pronounced either as a soft ц—цярь 'tsar', цяшка 'cup' —or as ч—чарь, чашка. Certain other variants are also possible.

From the grammatical point of view the northern dialects are characterised by the following features:

(1) by the forms меня, тебя, себя—in contrast to South Russian мене, тебе, себе;

(2) by the hard final т in the third person of the present tense—идет, идут, and not идеть, идуть;

(3) by the dative and instrumental case being identical in the plural—обзавестись сапогам 'to get oneself fitted out with boots', гулять с девушкам 'go out with girls';

(4) by the comparative degree in—яе—красняе 'redder', скоряе 'quicker';

(5) by the use of the postpositive particle after the noun—дом-от, изба-та, сено-то, люди-те (or люди-ти);[1]

(6) by impersonal constructions with passive participles, e.g. у них хожено—instead of они ходили 'they went';

(7) by such constructions with the gerund as он вышедши instead of он вышел 'he went out';

(8) by the use of the nominative singular of feminine nouns (instead of the accusative) as the direct object with an infinitive, e.g. принести книга 'to bring a book', напоить корова 'to give water to the cow'.

In the realm of vocabulary too there are many features peculiar to the northern dialects, e.g. орать 'to plough' [пахать in the literary language], but пахать meaning 'to sweep'; зевать meaning 'to cry, shout' [instead of 'to yawn']; лонись 'last year'; баско for красиво; бороновать 'to harrow', and not as in the south скородить; ухват instead of рогач for 'oven rake'; and many others.

The southern dialects include those of Tula, Kaluga (bordering on Belorussian), Orel, Kursk, the Don, Voronezh, the southern part of Ryazan' and the lower Volga. The salient features of southern speech are as follows.

The main feature of pronunciation is that the quality of a vowel depends on whether it is stressed or unstressed. This gives rise to аканье, which means that in unstressed syllables there is no difference between the vowels written о and а. Instead of these two vowels in unstressed positions various vowels occur—a more or less pure *a*, a sound between *a* and *ы*, etc. The exact pronunciation depends upon a variety of specific conditions, differing in various dialect groups. In any case, the essential feature of all these varieties of аканье is the absence in pronunciation of an unstressed vowel о, and its constant identification with the vowel *a*, the same substitute standing for both. Thus, in the south, for вода and трава they say in some places вада,

---

[1] The meaning of this may be compared with that of the definite article in English. [Ed.]

трава́, in others въда́, тръва́ (ъ here representing a sound intermediary between *a* and *ы*), the exact quality of the vowel varying from one group of dialects to another, and in dependence upon its position in the word. In addition to а́канье, mention must also be made of я́канье, which is the identical pronunciation of the vowels *a* (orthographically—я) and *e* in an unstressed position after a soft consonant. In some southern dialects for пята́к 'five-copeck coin' and беда́ 'trouble' they say пята́к, бяда́; in others—пита́к, бида́; in a third group—пита́к, бида́, but e.g. [with и or ы following] пяти́, бяды́; in a fourth—пята́к, бяда́, but [before a soft consonant] пити́ 'five', биде́. The exact pronunciation depends on various specific circumstances, but the result is always that there is no difference between the sounds written *a* and *e* after soft consonants in an unstressed position.

The other most important phonetic trait of southern dialects is the fricative г, articulated like x, but voiced, e.g. [ɣa'ra] гора́, ['ɣorat] or ['ɣorət] го́род, etc.

From the point of view of grammar the southern Russian dialects are characterised by:

(1) the soft final т in third person forms of the verb—идеть, идуть;

(2) the forms мене́, тебе́, себе́ [for меня́, тебя́, себя́];

(3) the frequent absence of the neuter gender, so that they say моя́ ведро́, све́жей ма́слы [for моё ведро́, све́жего ма́сла];

(4) and the fact that the short form of the adjective has become almost extinct.

Words characteristic of south Russian dialects include: скороди́ть instead of борорнова́ть 'to harrow'; рога́ч and not ухва́т 'oven rake'; ло́шадь and not конь for 'horse'; etc.

Finally we come to the middle Russian dialects, which extend in a band between the northern and southern dialects from north-west to south-east, i.e. approximately from Pskov province through the Moscow region to the lower Volga. These dialects are marked by a characteristic combination of the features of the northern and southern dialects. They have obviously been produced by the mixing of people from the northern and southern dialect areas to form a separate ethnographical entity. One of the typical products of this dialectal crossing in the middle Russian zone are dialects characterised by the southern pronunciation of vowels and the northern pronunciation of consonants. This means they have аканье, but also the plosive [g] and not [ɣ], the hard т in the third person of the present tense of the verb and so on. In middle Russian we find, for example, гара́, corresponding to the northern гора́ and the southern ɣапа́. This system of pronunciation is in fact characteristic of the Moscow dialect on which the Russian literary language was based. From authentic sources we know that the Moscow dialect formerly retained the pronunciation of o in unstressed positions (*о́канье*). Thus the modern middle Russian pronunciation of the Moscow variety is historically a northern pronunciation in which *оканье* has been replaced by the аканье of the south.

Irrespective of the differences between the various groups, all Russian dialects share certain general features which distinguish them from the dialects of the Ukraine and Belorussia. One such specifically Russian feature is the development of the sounds o and e from the original ы and и in the position before й, e.g. слепо́й 'blind', мой 'my', пей 'drink', as compared with Ukrainian сліпи́й, мий, пий[1] and Belorussian сляпы́, мый, пій. Another feature which has already been mentioned is the elimination of the old consonant mutations in declension, where velars were replaced by sibilants, so that modern Russian has на ноге́, в руке́, о грехе́ instead of Old Russian на нозѣ, въ руцѣ, о грѣсѣ. These mutations have been retained till the present day in Ukrainian and Belorussian, e.g. нозі—назе, etc. Here too we must mention the loss of the vocative case in Russian, the development of plural forms of the type города́ which are unknown in Ukrainian and Belorussian, and various other phenomena. On the other hand, certain developments common to Ukrainian and Belorussian dialects are completely absent from Russian, e.g. Ukrainian крива́вий, 'bloody', дрижа́ти 'tremble', and Belorussian крыва́вы, дрыжа́ць, as compared with Russian крова́вый, дрожа́ть; Ukrainian судця́, Belorussian судзя́ 'judge' [with double consonants] as compared with Russian судья́. All such phenomena affecting the interrelationship among Russian dialects and their relationship to those of the Ukraine and Belorussia must be taken into account in any attempt to explain historically the present-day state of the East Slavonic language area.

Unfortunately no fully reliable and clear answer has yet been

---

[1] The letter и in Ukrainian represents a vowel somewhere between Russian ы and French *é*, which does not soften a preceding consonant. [Ed.]

found to the question of how the present distribution of the East Slavonic languages came about. In recent times a very interesting and relatively detailed account has been put forward by the eminent scholar Shakhmatov. His idea of the origin of the East Slavonic dialects, brilliantly and persuasively set out in its final form in 1916, can be summarised as follows:

In the epoch preceding the rise of the Kievan state there were three groups of eastern Slavonic dialects: northern, southern and eastern. The tribes speaking the northern dialects were the Slovene[1] of Lake Il'men' (ильме́нские славя́не or слове́не) and the neighbouring Krivichi (кривичи́) (северя́не) Severyane. The southern dialects were spoken by the Polyane (поля́не), Drevlyane (древля́не), and the tribes settled to the west and south-west of them—the Volhynians (волы́няне), the people living on the river Bug (бужа́не), the Duleby (дуле́бы), the Tivertsy (ти́верцы), and the Ulichi (у́личи). The eastern dialects were used by the Vyatichi (вя́тичи) who lived in the basin of the river Oka, but according to Shakhmatov may well have had settlements as far south as the lower course of the Don. The western territory of European Russia, lying between the settlements of the southern and northern group, were, Shakhmatov supposed, occupied originally by Polish tribes. He considered the Dregovichi (дрегови́чи) and the Radimichi (ради́мичи) mentioned in the chronicles to be of Polish stock. The military and political impacts which Kievan Rus' experienced from early times as the consequence of repeated movements of nomads invading from the east and south-east, led to various movements of the eastern Slavonic tribal groupings and to their becoming mixed with each other. Thus some southern tribes were forced to cross their natural frontier, the River Pripyat', and as a result came in contact with the Polish tribes who were already there. On the other hand groups of eastern Slavs fleeing from the devastation of the Pechenegs, Polovtsy and Tatar hordes moved in that same direction.[2] Thus as a result of the simultaneous influences from south and east, the Polish tribes living in the territory

---

[1] Not to be confused with the Slovenes of Yugoslavia. [Ed.]

[2] The Pechenegs (печене́ги) were a nomadic people of Turkic origin from Central Asia who in the 8th and 9th centuries appeared in the steppes between the lower reaches of the Volga and the Yaik and made frequent attacks on Kievan Rus'. In the 11th century they were driven to the west and partly absorbed by the Polovtsy (по́ловцы), also of Turkic origin. Rus' carried on an unsuccessful struggle against the Polovtsy who, in the 13th century, were in their turn conquered by the Mongols and became absorbed into the Golden Horde.

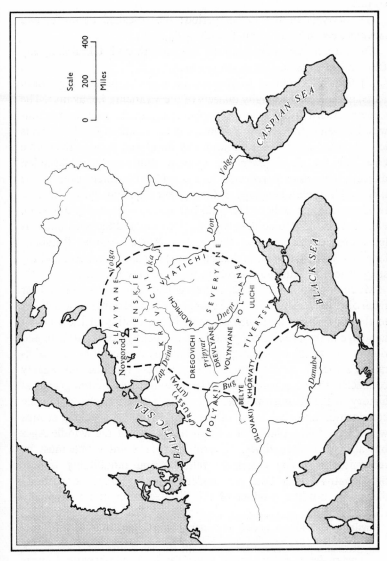

Probable approximate location of the East Slavonic tribes in the 9th century A.D.

later to be known as Belorussia underwent Russianisation. In modern Belorussian Shakhmatov accordingly noted three separate strata:

(1) survivals of the Polish period: the so-called *dzekanie*, and *tsekanie*, e.g. цёплы, дзень for тёплый, день;

(2) features common both to Belorussian and Ukrainian, e.g. Belorussian суддзя, Ukrainian суддя:

(3) features common to Belorussian and the present-day south Russian dialects (originally dialects of the Vyatichi), i.e. аканье. The same southern tribes whose settlements lay to the west and south-west of the central Kievan provinces later colonised the Kiev lands left neglected after the depredations of Batu[1] and became the ethnic basis for the development of modern south-western Ukrainian dialects. This basis is reflected to a considerable extent even in the literary Ukrainian language of the present day. Finally, the eastern tribes moved not only to the west, but also in a northerly direction. Here they came into contact with the Krivichi and Slovene, and this led to the development of the modern Russian (Great Russian)[2] language with its two basic dialects—northern and southern, and the strip of middle Russian dialects in the area between them.

Much of Shakhmatov's exposition is based on audacious and far from obvious assumptions. The exaggerated importance he attributes to the part played by Polish elements in the destiny of the Russian language in the pre-literary period has frequently been criticised, and rightly so. On the other hand, even if all the propositions of Shakhmatov's theory were accepted it nevertheless remains but weakly connected to the concrete facts of the political and ethnographical history of the Russian people, and to the numerous changes in the composition and settlements of the diverse Russian-speaking groups which have taken place not only in the course of the Middle Ages but also in modern times. Nevertheless one point which must be recognised as being extremely valuable and indubitably true is Shakhmatov's idea that the modern Russian language with its dialects is not the product of the disintegration of an originally

---

[1] Batu was a Mongol–Tatar khan, grandson of Genghis Khan. He conquered Russia in 1236–40 and made it a tributary of the Golden Horde. [Ed.]

[2] The term Great-Russian (великору́сский) is sometimes used to denote specific-ally Russian matters as distinct from White Russian (better called Belorussian to avoid confusion with politically 'White' Russians) and Ukrainian, formerly called by the Russians 'Little Russian' (малоросси́йский). [Ed.]

united whole into two separate groups. On the contrary, it is the product of the crossing of two formerly independent dialectal groups, brought together by a chain of historical events which made the centre of European Russia the vital centre of the future Russian state. At this place where the north and east Russian dialects met, the first threads in the fabric of a common Russian language were woven, to produce the central Russian transitional dialects. The subsequent extension of the middle Russian dialect region was a manifestation of the ever-growing bonds between the constituent parts of this new linguistic formation, the history of which is characterised by a marked tendency towards centralisation. Another result of this complicated process was the Moscow dialect, which in its capacity as the dialect of the capital and of the cultural centre of the Russian state, acquired particular importance. Thus an extremely important principle in the history of the Russian language is established, namely that the features common to the northern and southern dialects of modern Russian are more recent than the points of difference between them. For example, the absence in modern Russian dialects of the old vocative case, or the occurrence of ой, ей in words like слепóй, пей—that is to say, the features characteristic of all the Russian dialects in contradistinction to Ukrainian and Belorussian, came into being later than such divergencies between the northern and southern dialects as the different pronunciations of г, оканье, аканье, etc.

The events which altered the prehistoric pattern of dialects as reconstructed by Shakhmatov, and have resulted in the modern grouping of East Slavonic dialects, took place during the 10th to 13th centuries. During this period the separate groups of Eastern Slavonic languages still continued to some extent to undergo processes common to all the dialects, but also developed in part those individual peculiarities which are the chief distinguishing features of the three modern East Slavonic languages. Therefore, when we use the term 'Russian language', we must distinguish two meanings in accordance with the two basic phases of the linguistic history of eastern Slavdom. Applied to the period up to the 13th and 14th centuries this term means the language of all the eastern Slavs as a whole, showing internal differences but representing a unity conditioned by a common political life within the framework of the Kievan state. As is well known the term 'Rus′' itself was originally applied to the state ruled by the descendants of Ryurik[1] and only later on came to be the designation of the newly formed state and nationality in the north-east. For the period after the 14th century, however, the term 'Russian language' is equivalent to the term 'Great-Russian' and distinguishes the Russian language in the modern sense from the languages of the Ukraine and Belorussia.

The processes in the development of the Eastern Slavonic language groups so far described do not explain the origins of the Russian literary language. This will be dealt with in the next chapter.

[1] Ryurik, d. 879—according to legend the leader of a group of Varangian (Viking) warriors 'called in' by the Slavs of Novgorod to rule as their prince from 862. [Ed.]

3

THE ORIGIN OF THE RUSSIAN
LITERARY LANGUAGE

As a result of the complex cultural, historical and political events which accompanied the spreading of Christianity in the Slav world, the language of the Eastern Slavs was committed to writing relatively late, only in the 10th century. The appearance of written literature[1] in various parts of the medieval world is clearly connected with the establishment of the Christian church. In his outstanding work on the history of the Greek language A. Meillet formulates this connection as follows:

After the rise of Christianity Greek became the language of the church only in those places where the people already spoke Greek. Whereas in the west, Latin, the language of the Roman empire, remained the official language of the church—the only language used in the liturgy, in the training of priests and for the propagation of knowledge—in the east there appeared as many literary languages of Christianity as there were nationalities which had attained self-awareness. The Holy Scriptures were translated into Gothic, Armenian, Coptic and Slavonic. For each of these vernaculars a well-adapted alphabet was created and a literary language evolved into which Greek works were translated and in which even original works were composed. Thus, whereas in the west Latin remained the sole language of religion and high intellectual culture, in the east there arose national ecclesiastical languages which became the languages of national cultures, some of which have been preserved till the present day.[2]

As Meillet further points out, all these national languages borrowed a great deal from Greek, since they received Christianity from the Greek and not the Roman source.

This can be compared with what Lomonosov wrote in 1755 about the significance of the Slavonic translation of the scriptures in the history of Russian, compared with the part played by Latin in Roman Catholic countries:

---

[1] Here, as frequently throughout this translation, the word 'literature' is used in the widest sense, corresponding to Russian 'письменность'—written texts of all kinds including e.g. letters and official documents—and not only 'literature' in the narrow sense of 'худóжественная литератýра'. [Ed.]

[2] A. Meillet, *Aperçu d'une histoire de la langue grecque*, 3rd ed., Paris, 1930, p. 305.

The origin of the Russian literary language

Those who look into ecclesiastical books written in the Slavonic tongue may see clearly how much of Greek richness there is in the Slavonic translation of the Old and New Testaments, the homilies of the Fathers, the hymns of the Damascenes and other canonical writers, and that from these we multiply the pleasantness of Russian speech, which is already great in its own abundance and apt for the acceptance of Greek beauty through the intermediary of Slavonic...The justice of this is proved by comparing Russian with other tongues related to it. The Poles, long adhering to the Catholic faith, conduct their service in the Latin language in which their hymns and prayers were composed in barbaric times, for the most part by inferior writers, and therefore they could not receive such advantages as our language has obtained from Greek. The German language was poor, simple and weak as long as Latin was used in the service. But when the German people began to read the sacred books and hear the service in their own language, then its richness increased and elegant writers appeared.

Although the two quotations above are so far apart both in time and in way of thought, nevertheless they contain the same idea, namely, that their dependence for their literary language upon the early translations of Christian liturgical works from Greek into Slavonic was beneficial for the Eastern Slavs and therefore for the Russians. The language of these translations is traditionally called Old Slavonic or Old Church Slavonic, and it arose as follows.

After the death of Charlemagne in the 9th century a powerful state arose in central Europe known as the Great Moravian Principality. The ruler of this Principality, a gifted statesman called Mojmir, was forced to carry on a constant struggle against the Germans, and in 846 was defeated by them. Mojmir's successor Rostislav, however, continued the struggle with considerable success. In order to oppose German pressure Rostislav resorted not only to armed force, but also to cultural measures. About 863 he sent an embassy to the Byzantine Emperor Michael III, requesting him to send to Moravia missionaries who could preach Christianity to the local population in its mother tongue. In this way Rostislav hoped to neutralise the influence of the German church (which used Latin) upon the political and cultural life of Moravia. The result of this initiative was the mission of the brothers Constantine and Methodius, one of the most important events in the cultural history of the whole Slav world.

Constantine (who on his deathbed took the monastic name Cyril)[1] and Methodius were sons of a Byzantine nobleman Leo. They lived in Salonika, and as there were many Bulgarian settlements in this

---

[1] He was subsequently canonised as St Cyril. [Ed.]

area, they were conversant with the local Macedonian dialect of Old Bulgarian. According to the original account, the Emperor Michael addressed the brothers before they set out for Moravia, in the following words: Ва бо еста [dual] селоунянина, да селоуняне вьси чисто словѣньски бесѣдоують,[1] that is: 'You belong to Salonika, and the people of Salonika all speak Slavonic well.' This practical knowledge of the language of the Salonika Bulgarians was the basis of the brothers' missionary activities.

Before they set out for Moravia, Constantine, a scholar of renown, invented a Slavonic alphabet and began translating the *Evangeliary*,[2] beginning with the words 'В начáле бы́ло слóво'—'In the beginning was the word'. In Moravia Constantine and Methodius completed this translation, and also trained priests for the national Slavonic church. After the death of the two brothers (Constantine died in 869, Methodius in 885), Rostislav's successor Svyatopolk abandoned the Slavonic liturgy in Moravia [in favour of Roman Catholic influence] and drove out the followers of Constantine and Methodius. The latter continued their translation work in Bulgaria, and here, especially during the reign of the Bulgarian Tsar Simeon at the beginning of the 10th century, the original translations were revised. These texts formed the basis for the development of written literature among the Slavs, and this process reached the Eastern Slavs also in the 10th century.

Despite the differences which must have existed between the Slavonic languages by the 9th and 10th centuries, they were still sufficiently similar to each other, especially in grammatical structure, for the written language created by Constantine and Methodius on the basis of a Bulgarian dialect to be acceptable not only in the western Slav world, in Moravia, but also at a later date among the eastern Slavs. Thus the language of the first translations became a kind of common literary language in the medieval Slav world, with a vocabularly drawn not only from Bulgarian, but including also a large number of western Slav elements, not to mention many borrowings from Greek and a certain number from Latin, etc. This Old Church Slavonic language was confined to books: no one used it in everyday speech. In each of the Slavonic countries where it was

[1] The characteristic spelling of солуняне and бесéдуют with oy was merely a convention copied directly from Byzantine Greek, and does not indicate a diphthong, but simply the sound *u*. [Ed.]
[2] Selections from the Gospels arranged for reading week by week. [Ed.]

used, initially in its capacity as the language of the church, and then as the language of culture in general, it differed to some extent from the living vernacular. These differences, however, were not sufficient to prevent its adoption in each country, and indeed it was Old Church Slavonic which, first in Moravia and then in Bulgaria, Serbia and Russia, created the conditions for the appearance of literate people and professional men of letters, and thus for the emergence of independent national literatures. It was precisely through the assimilation and copying out of Old Church Slavonic texts that Old Russian literature came into being.

The translations of Constantine and Methodius, while they do have certain shortcomings, are on the whole of considerable literary quality. (They have come down to us not in the original form, but in later copies and recensions belonging to the 10th and 11th centuries.) One of the factors which gave them enormous cultural importance for the Slavs was that they brought the Slavonic world into communion with Byzantine literature, which despite its idiosyncrasies was still closely linked with the Classical tradition. The lexical, phraseological and syntactical Hellenisms in which Old Church Slavonic texts abound were assimilated without detriment to the national character of the emerging literary languages of the Slavonic countries, and not only gave to these languages a rightful place in the international linguistic community of the Middle Ages, but contributed considerably to the development of literature in these languages. As we saw above, this was already understood by Lomonosov so far as Russian was concerned. Pushkin later developed the same idea, writing in 1825:

As a vehicle for literature the Slavonic-Russian language [that is, the literary language that developed in Russia through the assimilation of Old Church Slavonic—the real history of the latter was not known to Pushkin and his contemporaries] enjoys an undoubted advantage over all European languages: fate was extremely kind to it. In the 11th century the ancient Greek language suddenly revealed to it the reasoned rules of its grammar, its fine turns of phrase and its majestic flow. In short, Greek adopted it, thus sparing it the necessity of waiting for the gradual improvements which come only with time. In itself Slavonic is sonorous and expressive, but it is indebted to Greek for its flexibility and regularity.

Later we shall attempt to trace the history of Old Church Slavonic on Russian soil and to clarify its role in the development of the Russian literary language. But our account of its beginnings would be

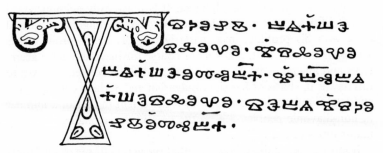

Glagolitic script from *Codex Zographensis*, reading: Искони бѣаше | слово и слово | бѣаше отъ б̄а (i.e. Бога) и б̄ъ (i.e. Богъ) бѣ-|аше слово себѣ иско-|ни отъ б̄а, the opening words of the Gospel according to St John.

Cyrillic uncial script from the *Ostromir Gospels*, giving basically the same text as above, except for the aorist бѣ instead of бѣаше.

incomplete without a reference to the great historical importance of Constantine's first achievement on behalf of Slavonic culture, namely the creation of a Slavonic alphabet. It is universally acknowledged that Cyril (i.e. Constantine) showed a remarkable linguistic flair and dealt with his problem in a masterly way. The best proof of his success is the fact that, allowing of course for inevitable later accretions and amendments, the alphabetic system he created survives to this day as the basis of Russian, Bulgarian and Serbian orthography, and is also reflected to a greater or lesser extent in that of a number of non-Slavonic peoples, e.g. in the present-day alphabets of many nationalities in the USSR.

It must be recognised, however, that the actual forms of the letters in the modern 'Cyrillic' alphabets in all probability do not derive from the alphabet invented by Cyril. The oldest extant texts in Church Slavonic are written in two different alphabets—Glagolitic and Cyrillic. The former is used, for instance, in the 11th-century manuscripts of the Gospels known as *Codex Zographensis* and *Codex Marianus*, the latter in the *Ostromir Gospels* of 1056, the 11th-century manuscript known as *Codex Supraslensis*, and others. Cyrillic, which was based on the formal Greek 'uncial' writing of the 8th–9th centuries, served in its turn as the basis of the modern Russian, Bulgarian and Serbian alphabets. Glagolitic, nowadays preserved only in the liturgy of the Roman Catholic Croats, can possibly be traced back to the Greek cursive handwriting of that period. In appearance Glagolitic differs vastly from Cyrillic, and only detailed analysis can reveal in its symbols a genetic relationship with Cyrillic and with the familiar forms of the Greek letters. It is interesting to note that the Cyrillic and Glagolitic symbols coincide mainly where they are derived not from Greek but from some other source (Coptic or perhaps Hebrew has been suggested), for example in the letter ш.

Which of the two Slavonic alphabets is the older, and therefore the one invented by Cyril? So far, no definitive answer has been given to this question. However, the overwhelming majority of scholars both in Slavonic and non-Slavonic countries have inclined to the opinion that Glagolitic was the earlier, and that Cyrillic originated only in the 10th century in Bulgaria, in connection with the revision of the translations of Constantine and Methodius carried out by their followers. The name of the inventor of the original Slavonic alphabet was subsequently transferred to this improved alphabet, in which, however, the principles behind the earlier one were in the vast majority of cases preserved. However, there is some reason for believing that at one time it was in fact Glagolitic that was called Cyrillic. Thus in 1047 the Novgorod priest Upyr′ Likhoy, in his epilogue to the manuscript of the Prophets with commentaries which he had written out, says: Сла́ва тебе́ го́споди царю́ небе́сный, я́ко сподоби мя написа́ти кни́гы сия́ ис коури́ловицѣ 'Glory be to Thee o Lord, King of Heaven, that Thou hast vouchsafed to me to write out these books from the Cyrillic'. Upyr′'s original manuscript has not come down to us, but copies of it belonging to the 15th century do contain words in the Glagolitic alphabet.We may therefore come to the plausible conclusion that what we now call Glagolitic, Upyr′ Likhoy called Cyrillic.

Glagolitic was not much used in ancient Rus′. There are no extant Old Russian manuscripts written entirely in Glagolitic. There are however Russian Cyrillic manuscripts in which isolated words and lines in Glagolitic occur, such as copies made from the already mentioned manuscript of Upyr′ Likhoy. There are also a few Glagolitic inscriptions on the walls of old Russian churches. Thus, so far as one can judge on the basis of extant Old Russian manuscript material, it seems likely that the direct source of the Russian literary language was not provided by the original Moravian texts, but by later texts from the Bulgarian period of Old Slavonic. N. K. Nikol′sky puts forward the very interesting hypothesis that the period of Byzantine–Bulgarian influence on Russian culture was preceded by a period of direct links with Moravian traditions, but that from the 11th century onwards scribes of a different persuasion deliberately obliterated traces of these traditions for tendentious reasons. Be that as it may, the Old Slavonic texts which entered the Eastern Slavonic world along with Christianity became models to be copied and imitated.

When copying Old Slavonic texts and composing original ones on Old Slavonic models, early Russian men of letters sometimes deviated, consciously or unconsciously, from the norms of Old Slavonic in favour of analogous forms drawn from their native speech. In this way Eastern Slavonic features were introduced into the orthography, grammatical system and vocabulary of the Old Slavonic originals. As a result there arose a distinctive, new literary language, which was a blend of elements of the bookish Old Slavonic and the living Eastern Slavonic language. It was this hybrid language, Old Church Slavonic in its Russian version, which became the first literary language of the Eastern Slavs. The same phenomenon is seen also in Bulgarian and Serbian in the 11th and 12th centuries, where vernacular elements appear in the basically older literary language of the original texts of Cyril and Methodius. Thus we can recognise not only Russian, but also Bulgarian and Serbian versions of Old Slavonic. There are also relics of a Moravian version in a few manuscripts, where features of the Moravian dialects have been introduced into the Salonikan–Macedonian language of Cyril and Methodius.

There exist certain external features which permit us to attribute a given Old Slavonic text to one or other of these variants. Two of these features will be mentioned here. In all the Slavonic languages in the pre-literary period there existed two nasal vowels ϱ and ϱ. These were denoted by the symbols known as 'юсы'—'big *yus*' (Cyrillic ѫ) to denote the nasal ϱ, and 'small *yus*' (Cyrillic ѧ) to denote the nasal ϱ. There were also two 'reduced vowels' in all the Slavonic languages at that period. These were pronounced extremely short and probably with a very slight vibration of the vocal cords (they are sometimes referred to as the 'voiceless' vowels). To denote these reduced vowels the Slavonic alphabet had two signs, the 'yers'— 'ep' for the back vowel (in Cyrillic ъ, i.e. the present-day hard sign), and 'ерь' for the front vowel (Cyrillic ь, i.e. the present-day soft sign). By the period from which the earliest extant Slavonic manuscripts date, i.e. towards the end of the 10th century and the beginning of the 11th, both the nasals and the reduced vowels had undergone certain changes in the various Slavonic languages. This gave rise to indecision about the spelling of words, and the characteristic use of the '*yuses*' and '*yers*' makes it possible to attribute manuscripts to one or other Slavonic area. Thus, it is characteristic of Bulgarian Old Slavonic to confuse 'big *yus*' with 'small *yus*' in certain positions, and '*yer*' with '*yer'*'. It is characteristic of the Serbian version to confuse the 'big *yus*' with the letter y, and the 'small *yus*' with the letter e, and to use ь instead of ъ. The Russian version is marked by the more or less correct use of ъ and ь, and, depending upon position, the confusion of 'big *yus*' with the letter y, and of 'small *yus*' either with a or with the so-called iotated a (ꙗ: Modern Russian я). Thus, for example, Old Slavonic ѧзыкъ (cf. Polish 'język') may appear in a Bulgarian manuscript as ѫзыкъ, in a Serbian manuscript as езикь, and in Russian as ꙗзыкъ.

The following brief extract from the *Archangel Gospels* will serve as an example of a Russian manuscript, at least part of which was written around 1092...(In the transcription of old texts from now on the orthography is slightly simplified, the abbreviations characteristic of medieval manuscripts (титлы) are expanded, and the letters ѧ and ꙗ replaced by я.)

Въ о́но врѣ́мя пришьдъшю іисоу́сови въ страну́ гергеси́ньскоу. съртѣ́оста и дъва бѣ́сьна. от жа́лии исходꙗ́ща. лю́тѣ зѣло́. ꙗ́ко не можꙗ́ше никто́ же миноу́ти поуть́мь тѣ́мь. и се възъпи́ста. глаго́люща. что есть на́ма іисоу́се и тебе́ сы́не бо́жии. пришь́лъ еси́ сѣ́мо прѣ́же врѣ́мене моу́читъ насъ. бѣ́ же далѣ́че отъ нею́ ста́до свини́и мъного пасо́мо. бѣси же молꙗ́хоути и глаго́люще. а́ще изго́ниши ны. повели́ намъ ити́ въ ста́до свино́е. и рече́ имъ иди́те. они́ же шь́дъше идо́шꙗ въ сви́ния. и а́бие оустрьми́ ся вьсе ста́до по бе́регоу. въ мо́ре и оутопо́шꙗ въ вода́хъ.

Literal translation from the Slavonic text: At that time Jesus coming to the Gergesene land, two men with demons met him coming out of the tombs, very wild, so that no one could pass that way, and they cried out saying, 'What are you to us, Jesus son of God? You have come before the time to torment us.' And there was a large herd of pigs grazing far from them. And the demons entreated him saying. 'If you drive us out, command us to enter into the herd of pigs.' And he said to them, 'Go', and they (going) went into the pigs. And immediately the whole herd dashed over the bank into the sea and drowned in the water. (Matt. 8. 28–32.)

Among the features indicating that this is a Russian text we may note въ страноу instead of въ странж in the original, and по берегоу instead of по брѣгоу.

Such simple examples demonstrate that the Old Russian literary language was essentially the product of hybridisation and amalgamation in which the two strains of the Slavonic book language and everyday Eastern Slavonic were mingled. However, the proportion of each of these basic elements in the amalgam varied with each individual case. This depended on the nature of the text being compiled, upon its content and style, upon the degree of erudition and culture of the scribe, his literary aims, and so on. Below we shall examine in greater detail the different types or styles of the Old Russian literary language which arose in this way, but as a preliminary we shall consider briefly the documents which we have at our disposal for reconstructing the history of the Russian language, particularly in the early period of its development.

4

TEXTS IN THE HISTORY

OF RUSSIAN

The most important category of texts for the history of Russian are manuscripts. Others, such as inscriptions on stones, coins and utensils, survive in very small numbers from the period when the language was first committed to writing, while those from later periods, because of their brevity, cannot compete in importance with manuscripts.

Of the inscriptions belonging to the earliest period, that on the Tmutorokan' stone is the best known. It is a piece of white marble discovered near Taman' in 1792, recording that in 1068 Prince Gleb measured the distance between Tmutorokan' and Kerch over the frozen Strait of Kerch, and found it to be 14,000 sazhens. Today this stone is preserved in the Hermitage Museum in Leningrad. There are no other inscriptions bearing dates of the 11th century, but four are ascribed to this period on indirect evidence. Altogether about a hundred and eighty inscriptions survive from the period from the 11th to the 14th century. Here, for example, is the text of an inscription on a silver goblet belonging to Prince Vladimir Davydovich of Chernigov (d. 1151), which is now kept in the Armoury Museum in Moscow (some of the words are incomplete):

А се чара кня Володимерова Давыдовча кто
из нее пь тому на здоровье а хваля бога
своего осподаря великого кня

This is the goblet of Volodimer Davydovich: he who drinks from it, good health to him and praising God...of his lord the Grand Prince...

There are considerably more examples of manuscripts dating as far back as the 11th century. The total number of manuscripts in existence from the period up to the reign of Peter I (1689–1725) runs into tens of thousands, but the vast majority of these are later than the 15th century. In all, about one thousand extant manuscripts

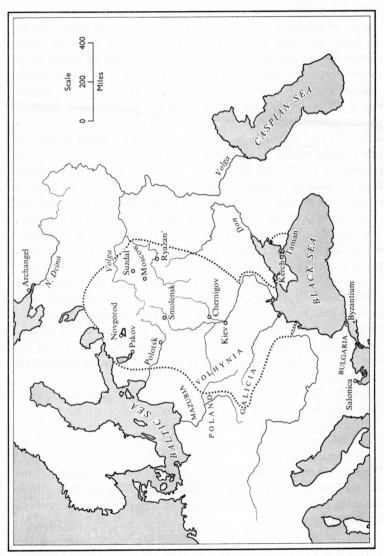

Medieval Russia. (··· Approximate extent of Kievan Rus' in the 11th century)

belong to the 11th to 14th centuries, and of these more than twenty are of the 11th century.

Till the middle of the 14th century all Russian manuscripts were written on parchment, but from the 15th century paper predominates (to begin with this was imported, but later Russian-made paper appeared). Manuscripts may be either in the form of books or of single-sheet documents.[1] There are several basic styles of handwriting: uncial, half-uncial and cursive. In the large and majestic uncial script (устáв) each architecturally proportioned letter is written separately. This script appears only in the very oldest manuscripts. From the middle of the 14th century the Russian half-uncial (полуустáв) makes its appearance, to be superseded in the 15th century by the Balkan half-uncial, borrowed, like so many things then fashionable in Russia, from Serbia and Bulgaria. Half-uncial script is less regular and calligraphic than uncial: straight lines are often replaced by sloping ones, and more abbreviations are used. The title of cursive script (скóропись) is self-explanatory. Its characteristic features are the linking together of letters, the variety of forms possible for the same letter, the freedom with which letters project above or below the line, the use of superscript letters, ligatures and abbreviations of various kinds. The old cursive hand differs from modern handwriting in allowing fewer personal idiosyncrasies, the various features mentioned above being subordinated to specific requirements of style. Some cursive manuscripts, especially of the late 16th and 17th centuries, are monuments of intricate and delicate calligraphy.

Finally, Old Russian manuscripts can be classified according to their contents into three basic categories:

(1) ecclesiastical literature,
(2) legal and business documents,
(3) literature proper.

We have examples of the first category from the 11th century, of the second from the 12th, and of the third chiefly from the 13th century onwards, although a few manuscripts of literary content exist which are of earlier date.

The earliest written records of Russian go back at least as far as

---

[1] 'Documents' is used here to translate the Russian word грáмоты, covering official, legal and personal writings ranging from charters and treaties to private letters and notes of business transactions. [Ed.]

Half-uncial script from a 16th-century manuscript, reading: И бяхоу вси людіе въ страсѣ велицѣ | оутѣсняеми. князь же великоде-|ржавный иже тогда скипетры роусь-|скихъ странъ обдержа. достохваль-|ный и побѣдоносный великый Дмитрей да глаголется...

And all the people were oppressed with great fear. But the mighty Prince who at that time held the sceptre of the Russian lands, to wit the praiseworthy and victorious great Dmitri...

Cursive from a 17th-century manuscript, reading: Гдрь црь (i.e. Государь царь) и великиі князь Алексѣй | Михаиловичь всеа Русиі по ихъ | челобитью велѣлъ ихъ приняти | во свою Государскую высокую руку...

The sovereign Tsar' and Grand Prince Aleksey Mikhaylovich of all Russia in accordance with their petition ordered them to be taken into his august regal hand...

the second decade of the 10th century. One of the *Chronicles* preserves the Russian text of the treaty drawn up between Oleg[1] and Byzantium in 912. The copies of the *Chronicle* containing the treaty, however, are not earlier than the 15th century. Not a single 10th-century manuscript has been preserved. So far as Old Russian literature (in the narrow sense) is concerned, there is no doubt that translations and original works already existed in the 11th century, but once again the oldest literary texts known to us are preserved only in copies of a later date. The copies of the *Chronicle* which we possess are no earlier than the 14th century, while *Слово о полку Игореве* (*The Tale of Igor's Host*) which was composed at the end of the 12th century, is known to us only in the printed edition of 1800 based on a 15th- or 16th-century manuscript.[2]

We shall mention below some of the best known and most valuable manuscripts of the Old Russian period. Those of the 11th century are chiefly liturgical or other ecclesiastical texts. All 11th-century Russian manuscripts are copies from Old Church Slavonic originals, and can be considered as texts of the Old Russian language on the whole only where they deviate from the linguistic norms of the original. The oldest of them, dated 1056–7, is known as *The Ostromir Gospels* (Остроми́рова Ева́нгелия) from the name of the Novgorodian governor (поса́дник) for whom it was made. It is a luxurious manuscript of large format consisting of 294 folios, written by several scribes in double-columns in a large formal uncial hand. The bulk of the work was carried out by the deacon Grigoriy, in whose name the traditional epilogue or colophon is written. The latter contains the customary address to the reader, asking him not to reproach the scribe for any errors he may have made: Да и́же гора́знѣе сего́ напи́ше, то не мози́ зазьрѣ́ти мьнѣ грѣ́шьникоу... молю́ же вьсѣ́хъ почита́ющихъ, не мозѣ́те кля́ти, нъ испра́вльше почита́ите. 'Let him who can write more skilfully not condemn me, sinner that I am...and I beg all those who may read, do not curse

---

[1] Oleg (d. 912 or 922), Prince of Kiev, who may be considered the real founder of Russia, gave it international status by negotiating by force of arms this advantageous commercial treaty, in which for the first time in any document the word *Rus'* appears. [Ed.]

[2] The *Slovo* was discovered in the 1790s by Count A. I. Musin-Pushkin among a number of manuscripts purchased from a monastery. In 1812 his house was destroyed in the burning of Moscow, and the manuscript lost. The authenticity of the *Slovo* has sometimes been questioned, most recently by A. Mazon and the Soviet scholar A. A. Zimin. [Ed.]

me, but make corrections as you read.' This colophon also informs us of the history of the manuscript and its date. It is a weekly Evangeliary, apparently copied for the most part direct from a Bulgarian original, but it seems likely that another intermediate Russian manuscript was used for some parts. The language is profoundly archaic, and frequently reflects the state of Old Slavonic at the time of Cyril and Methodius better than any other Slavonic texts. It does however contain distinct traces of Eastern Slavonic speech. In all probability the manuscript was written in Kiev, but it contains no specific dialect features. The *Ostromir Gospels* have played a particularly important role in the development of Russian and Slavonic philology, since it was on this text that the outstanding scholar A. Kh. Vostokov at the beginning of the 19th century based his pioneering work in this field. In 1843 he published an excellent printed edition of this manuscript, furnished with a glossary and paradigms.

Next in chronological order mention must be made of two copies of *Svyatoslav's Miscellanies* (*Избо́рники Святосла́ва*), one of 1073 and the other of 1076, which take their name from Svyatoslav, Grand Prince of Kiev, to whose library they belonged. These are collections of various works of Byzantine literature, mainly of an edifying, didactic nature, which were translated [from Greek] for the Bulgarian Tsar Simeon in the 10th century. The Russian *Изборники* were copied from these Bulgarian originals. It is significant that the earlier one contains a treatise on 'creative images' (*О обра́зѣхъ*) expounding certain principles of Byzantine poetic theory which were doubtless of value to the first Russian writers.

The *Archangel Evangeliary* (*Арха́нгельское Ева́нгелие*) of 1092 derives its name from the fact that it was discovered in the 1880s in Archangel. The provenance of this manuscript is still unclear, but it seems probable that it originated in the south. This is again a weekly Gospel, written out by two scribes who, however, lapsed more frequently than deacon Grigoriy from the strict norms of Old Church Slavonic into their native Russian. It is therefore of great linguistic value, and an excellent facsimile edition was printed in Moscow in 1912.

Other dated texts of the 11th century are the *Novgorod Minei* (*Новгоро́дские служе́бные мине́и*)[1] of 1095 and subsequent years.

[1] The menology (from Greek *menaios* 'monthly') was a popular form of work consisting of a calendar of feast days with lives of the saints of the Orthodox church. [Ed.]

3-2

These texts, which have not yet been published in full, are copies from Bulgarian originals which were themselves translations from Greek. The 11th century *Minei* are of especial interest because they reproduce peculiarities of the old Novgorod dialect. The most characteristic of these is цóканье—the regular confusion of ц and ч, so that on, the one hand, письчь and личе are written instead of пи́сьць 'writer' and ли́це 'face', but црѣвѣ and пецаль appear instead of чрѣвѣ 'belly, womb' and печа́ль 'sadness'. These spellings undoubtedly represent a type of pronunciation of Russian which does not differentiate between ц and ч (cf. p. 12).

The most important 12th-century ecclesiastical text is *Mstislav's Gospels* (*Мстисла́вово Ева́нгелие*) written before 1117. There are also two texts reflecting the dialect of Galicia–Volhynia—the *Galician Gospels* (*Га́лицкое Ева́нгелие*) of 1144, and *Dobrilov's Gospels* (*Добри́лово Ева́нгелие*) of 1164. The latter is of particular importance for the history of Ukrainian because of A. I. Sobolevsky's discovery, made in the 1880s, that it contains specifically Ukrainian phonetic features. The colophon with its familiar theme indicates the spirit in which the actual process of transcription went on: А бра́тья и отьци́, а́же вы кде кри́во а испра́вивъше чьтѣ́те а не кльнѣ́те я́ко же ра́дуеться жени́хъ о невѣ́стѣ та́ко ра́доуеться пи́сець ви́дя послѣ́дьнии листъ. 'Brothers and fathers, if it is distorted in places then correct as you read and blame not; as the bridegroom rejoices in his bride so the scribe rejoices seeing the last page.' Compare the colophon from the Laurentian copy[1] of the *Chronicle* (1377): Ра́дуется купе́ць прику́пъ створи́въ. и ко́рмьчии въ оти́шье приста́въ и стра́нникъ въ оте́чьство свое́ пришé́дъ. та́коже ра́дуется и кни́жный списа́тель. дошéдъ конца́ кни́гамъ 'The merchant rejoices having made a bargain, the helmsman heaving to in calm water, and the traveller returning to his native land, so also rejoices the scribe reaching the end of his books'.

The language of the 12th century has also come down to us through several manuscripts which are not copies, but original Russian texts. We possess two brief 12th-century documents, both deeds of gift, the one on behalf of the Grand Prince Mstislav and his son Vsevolod addressed to the Yur'ev monastery in Novgorod about 1130, the other from the end of the century addressed to the Khutyn monastery by its founder, the monk Varlaam. Although the latter is

---

[1] Named after the scribe Lavrentiy. [Ed.]

short, it contains many clear examples of north Russian dialect forms.

Finally, from the 12th century onwards we have copies of original Russian literary works, for instance the *Miscellany* of the Uspensky Cathedral in Moscow (*Сборник московского Успенского собора*), *c.* 1190, which contains among other things the oldest version of the popular *Legend of Saints Boris and Gleb*[1] (*Сказание о Борисе и Глебе*), and also the *Life of Feodosiy of the Monastery of the Caves* (*Житие Феодосия Печерского*). Altogether more than fifty 12th-century manuscripts are extant.

[An important new source for the history of the language used in everyday affairs was provided in 1951–8 by the discovery, during excavations in Novgorod, of large numbers of documents written on pieces of birch-bark (берестяные грамоты), ranging in date from the 11th to the 15th century. Ed.]

There is a considerable number of manuscripts dating from the 13th and 14th centuries associated with the various cultural centres of medieval Russia, e.g. documents from Smolensk (the oldest 1229), Novgorod (the oldest 1262), Moscow (the oldest being the testament of Ivan Kalita, 1328),[2] Ryazan' (the oldest 1356), etc. Many valuable documents written in the region of the Northern Dvina in the 15th century have been preserved. The most outstanding legal text of the 13th century is the oldest extant copy of the *Russian Law* (*Русская правда*)[3] written out in the area of Novgorod in 1282. This law code was composed much earlier, and copies must certainly have been in circulation in the first half of the 11th century. It is possible that the first part of the oldest extant copy of the Old Russian chronicles, the Synodal manuscript of the *Novgorod Primary Chronicle* (*Первая Новгородская летопись*), belongs to the end of the 13th century, but without any doubt the greater part of it was copied in the 14th century. The famous Laurentian copy of the *Chronicle*, dated 1377, was copied in the Suzdal' region, and in

[1] Two of the many sons of Grand Prince Vladimir of Kiev, who were murdered in 1015 by their brother Svyatopolk, and subsequently canonised as the first Russian saints because of their submissive acceptance of suffering. [Ed.]

[2] Ivan I, Grand Prince of Moscow 1325–40, nicknamed 'moneybag' because of his astute policies which enriched Moscow and strengthened it against the Tatars. [Ed.]

[3] The legal code compiled by Yaroslav the Wise (978–1054), Grand Prince of Kiev. [Ed.]

addition to the *Пóвесть временнЫх лет* (*Tale of Bygone Years*)[1] composed in the South in the 12th century, contains another local Suzdal' chronicle. Many other valuable copies of the *Chronicle*, including the Hypatian (Ипáтьевская), Radziwill or Königsberg manuscripts, are ascribed to the 15th century. Certain works of Old Russian literature are preserved in 13th-century copies, e.g. the splendid sermons of [Bishop] Kirill of Turov and the translation of the Byzantine *Chronicle of George Hamartolos* (*ХрóникA Геóргия Амáртола*). We have to rely on later manuscripts for copies of other literary texts, e.g. *Слóво о закóне и благодáти* (*Homily on Law and Grace*) by Ilarion[2] which belongs to the 11th century but is known in its entirety only from a 16th-century copy, and *Слóво о полкý Йгореве*. The late date of the manuscripts constitutes a great disadvantage in analysing these works from the linguistic point of view.

However, the position becomes much easier from the 15th century onwards. The most important literary works of the Muscovite period are known to us in copies more or less contemporary with their actual composition, e.g. *Задóнщина* [a heroic account of the Battle of Kulikovo, 1380, in which Grand Duke Dmitriy 'Donskoy' won an important victory over the Tatars], Afanasiy Nikitin's *Хожéния за три мóря* [an account by a merchant of Tver' of his travels in 1466–72 which took him as far as India], the correspondence between Ivan IV 'the Terrible' and Prince Andrey Kurbskiy [1563–79], *Домострóй* [a mid-16th-century treatise on the proper running of a household which has become a symbol of Muscovite ideology], *Стоглáв* [the 'hundred sections' of the report drawn up in 1551 by a council of the Orthodox church held in Moscow to consider questions of ritual, administration, etc.], Kotoshikhin's *Запúски* [an account written in 1666–7 by an émigré of Russian life and institutions], the works of Avvakum [Archpriest and leader of the schismatic Old Believers, burned at the stake in 1682, who is known chiefly for his autobiography], the Law Code (*Уложéние*) of 1649, and various narratives and legends, some translated or adapted from foreign sources, others original Russian works.

From the 17th century we have several printed books, printing

---

[1] An account of the history of the Eastern Slavs from the Flood to the 12th century, long attributed to the Kievan monk Nestor. [Ed.]

[2] A theological discussion on the Old and New Testaments written somewhere between 1040 and 1050 by Ilarion, the first Russian-born Metropolitan of Kiev. [Ed.]

having been introduced into Russia in the second half of the 16th century.[1] To begin with only ecclesiastical books were printed, but in 1647 the first secular text appeared—*Уче́ние и хи́трость ра́тного строе́ния пехо́тных люде́й* (*The Science and Art of Military Formation in the Infantry*). This was printed in Moscow, and was followed by a Church Slavonic grammar in 1648, and the Law Code in 1649. From about the end of the 17th century the printing of secular works became a regular occurrence. Even after this date manuscripts continue to be an important source for the history of the language, but printed books assume an ever-increasing import- ance. The chief value of manuscripts then becomes that of providing original versions with which printed texts can be collated.

Throughout the Old Russian period we can observe in the written works a struggle between centripetal and centrifugal tendencies. Sometimes features of the living language break the surface of the text, and sometimes they are obscured by a more or less consistent observance of the grammatical norms of Church Slavonic. This makes the study of Russian historical dialectology extremely difficult, and it is not surprising that we still cannot establish a clear and compre- hensive picture of the evolution of the Old Russian dialects in their successive stages. However, we do have a good idea of some of the most important features of certain regional dialects of medieval Russia. It was mentioned above that Sobolevsky established certain specific linguistic features of Galician–Volhynian texts of the 12th century. He was also the first person to describe the language of texts written in the area of Pskov, which possesses a number of very characteristic features. The most striking of these is the lack of distinction between hissing and 'hush' sibilants, betrayed in writing by the confusion of the letters с and ш, з and ж, e.g. сапо́зник instead of сапо́жник 'cobbler', but сапожи́ instead of сапози́ 'boots' [old nominative plural with second palatalisation—cf. p. 5. Ed.]; or обѣ́давсю instead of обѣ́давшю [past participle passive of обѣ́дать], but еши́ instead of еси́ 'thou art'. In a well-known passage of *Сло́во о полку́ Игореве* we find шизымъ орломъ подъ облакы 'like a grey eagle beneath the clouds' with ши́зымъ instead of the expected си́зымъ, which leads some scholars to conclude that the Musin- Pushkin manuscript of the *Сло́во о полку́ Игореве* must have been

[1] The earliest (dated) Russian printed book was the *Апостолъ* printed in Moscow in 1564 by Ivan Fyodorov. [Ed.]

39

written in or near Pskov. The peculiarity we have just mentioned appears not only in the old Pskov dialect, but also in the Mazurian dialects of Polish, and it seems probable that we can postulate a common substratum of some other language. It has been suggested by A. M. Selishchev that this confusion of sibilants is characteristic of Polonised or Russianised speakers of the Old Prussian language (an extinct language of the Baltic group related to Lithuanian and Lettish). Selishchev traced to this same source another unique feature of the old Pskov dialect, namely the appearance in the past tense forms of the combinations гл and кл, where modern Russian has simply л, e.g. блюглися instead of блюлися [from блюстись 'to be preserved'], or чкли instead of чли [from честь 'to consider']. Neither of these features appears in modern Pskov dialects.

Similarly, certain dialect features occur in manuscripts originating in Smolensk-Polotsk, the Northern Dvina region, Ryazan', Moscow, etc. The reflection of аканье in Moscow documents is particularly significant, and appears only from a very late date. For instance, there are no traces of it in the writings of Ivan IV [1530–84], but we constantly find in the letters of Tsar′ Aleksey Mikhaylovich [1629–76] such spellings as по палямъ (по поля́м), десять утакъ (у́ток), and conversely выто́щили (вы́тащили). We may therefore surmise that the tremendous social upheavals which took place at the end of the 16th and beginning of the 17th centuries brought about a considerable change in the language of the Muscovite ruling class, and that it is to this period that we must trace the change in the Moscow dialect from the оканье of the Northern dialects to Central Russian аканье (cf. chapter 2).

5

THE STRUCTURE OF OLD RUSSIAN

The language of the oldest written Russian texts, despite their variations in dialect and style, and in the extent to which they comply with the norms of Old Church Slavonic, reflects certain general features of the Eastern Slavonic language system, and a chronological study of these texts reveals how this system has changed to produce the modern language. Below we shall consider the most important phonological and grammatical features of Eastern Slavonic, reconstructed on the basis of these texts.

The system of vowel sounds differed from that of modern Russian by possessing the sounds represented by the letters ѣ, ъ and ь. The letter ѣ (called ять) denoted a sound similar to e, but differing from the e of modern Russian in two respects. Firstly, it was a long vowel (but this quality was lost at an early period), and secondly, it was narrow, i.e. pronounced with the blade of the tongue in a higher position, giving a sound intermediate between *e* and *i*. It seems probable that the nearest analogy to the original sound of ѣ in modern Russian is the sound used in words where ѣ formerly appeared, in the Northern dialects of the White Sea and Vyatka regions (cf. p. 12). In certain other dialects in place of the old ѣ in stressed positions a characteristic compound sound occurs, starting like *i* and finishing as *e*, i.e. something like лиес, миел, диевка [for лес, мел, дѐвка]. Some scholars consider that this was precisely how ѣ sounded in the original Russian dialects. Subsequently ѣ in most cases came to coincide either with e (as in Belorussian and modern standard Russian) or with и (as in Ukrainian and sometimes in North Russian dialects—cf. p. 12). It must be noted that in the earliest form of the written language the letters ѣ and e stood for sounds which differed sufficiently to distinguish words of different meaning which were otherwise identical in sound [i.e. they were separate phonemes. Ed.]. Thus there existed such pairs of words as ѣли 'ate' and éли 'fir trees', сѣла 'sat' and сéла

41

'villages',[1] рѣчи́ 'speech' (prepositional case) and речи́ 'to speak' (infinitive).

The sounds represented by the symbols ъ ('*yer*') and ь ('*yer'*'), were extremely short, 'reduced' vowels, the quality of the former being between *o* and *u*, and that of the latter between *e* and *i*. It was mentioned above that these vowels were probably pronounced with very little voice. Both of them occur very frequently in the language of the earliest period, and there are many Old Russian words in which there are no vowels other than ъ and ь, e.g. сънъ (сон 'sleep'), сънъмь (сном—instrumental singular of сон), сънъмъ (сонм 'multitude'), ръпътъ (ро́пот 'murmur'), дьнь (день 'day'), жьньць (жнец 'reaper'), жьрьць (жрец 'priest'), съмьрть (смерть 'death'), кръшькъ (кро́шек 'crumbs'—genitive plural of кро́шка). The present-day reader must accustom himself to the idea that these symbols represented vowel sounds which were pronounced wherever they occurred, even at the end of a word.[2] Thus such words as кръшькъ, жьрьцъ and жьньць had three syllables, while the instrumental singular of жьрьць—жьрьцьмь—had four. Subsequently, in certain positions in a word the sounds ъ and ь were either replaced by *o* and *e* respectively, or disappeared completely. A consonant which had originally been followed by the vowel ь remained soft, and the symbol was frequently preserved in the spelling, now, however, being simply a 'soft sign' and not a vowel symbol. Thus, for instance, the Old Russian disyllable дьнь became the monosyllable день, in which the ь merely indicates that the н is palatalised.

Among other things, the disappearance of the *yers* or their replacement by *o* and *e* led to the characteristic feature of modern Russian known as the fleeting vowel—the large number of words in which one grammatical form contains the vowel *o* or *e*, while another does not, e.g. сон—сна (formerly съна), кро́шек—кро́шка (formerly кръшька), сильна́—силён (formerly сильнъ). In fact these changes, which took place in the Eastern Slavonic dialects in the 11th and 12th centuries, radically altered the whole vowel system of Russian. It was as a result of this process that it again became possible to have closed syllables, which had been lost in all the Slavonic languages in the pre-literary period (cf. p. 4). Contrast e.g. сънъ which has two

---

[1] It was not until later that *e* in stressed positions came to be pronounced as *o* (сёла)—cf. pp. 44, 70. [Ed.]

[2] It is also noteworthy that these 'reduced' vowels could nevertheless be stressed, e.g. сънъмь. [Ed.]

syllables each ending in a vowel, with modern сон with one syllable ending in a consonant. In addition various consonant clusters which had formerly been impossible now appeared, e.g. modern Russian пчела́ 'bee', жбан 'pitcher', три́жды 'thrice', from Old Russian бьчела, чьбанъ, тришьды.

By the time when the language was first written down, the Eastern Slavs had already lost the nasal vowels ρ and ϱ, which had formerly existed in all the Slavonic languages. The nasal ρ was replaced by u, and ϱ by a combined with palatalisation of the preceding consonant (cf. p. 8). In medieval Russian manuscripts this led to the peculiarly Russian version of the Church Slavonic language described in chapter 3. Since they had no nasal vowels in their own language, the creators of the Russian literary language reading the Old Slavonic texts took the symbol ж to signify the sound u (which in Old Slavonic, following the Greek convention, was represented by the two letters oy) and ѧ as the sound a following a soft consonant (whereas the symbol for this in Old Slavonic was а or ꙗ 'iotated a'). Thus the Old Russian scribes had no criteria for differentiating between ж and oy, or between ѧ and ꙗ(а), and in copying from Old Slavonic texts they freely substituted one for the other. Thus, for example, in the *Ostromir Gospels* we find водоу instead of the correct Old Slavonic accusative form водж 'water'; and држже instead of дроуже 'friend' (vocative); глаголꙗ instead of глаголѧ 'saying' (gerund); and морѧ instead of морꙗ 'seas', etc.... The symbol ж was discarded in Russian manuscripts in the middle of the 12th century, but later, during the second period of Southern Slavonic influence in the 15th century, its use was revived for a time. The symbol ѧ, in the modified form я, has been preserved to this day.

One further peculiarity of Old Russian phonology must be mentioned: the fact that at that time the velar consonants г, к and х could be followed by the vowel ы, e.g. гыбель, кыслыи, хытрыи [modern Russian ги́бель 'doom', ки́слый 'sour', хи́трый 'cunning']; while, as in all the Slavonic languages, these consonants never appeared before the vowel и, since [because of the first and second palatalisations, Ed.] in such a position they had changed respectively to the sibilants ж or з, ч or ц, ш or с. From the 12th century, however, manuscripts indicate that the pronunciation гы, кы, хы was beginning to be replaced, first of all in specific regions, but later throughout the Russian-speaking area, by ги, ки, хи. Thus we begin to find the spelling княги́ня instead of княгы́ня 'princess', па́ки instead of пакы 'again', Ки́евъ instead of Кыевъ, etc. It must also be noted that in Old Russian the hush-sibilants ж, ш, щ and ч, and the affricate ц were originally palatalised consonants. In modern standard Russian щ and ч remain soft, but since approximately the 14th–15th centuries ж, ш, and ц have become hard consonants. The soft pronunciation of ж and ш which occurs today in a few dialects (e.g. before и and е in Vyatka) is a relic of the older system. The other consonants could be either hard or soft—originally hard before back vowels and soft before front vowels. Three consonants, н, р and л were exceptional in that they could be palatalised even before а and у.[1]

Originally the combination of a soft consonant and the vowel *o* was impossible in Russian, so that in Old Russian the letter е in such words as желоудь 'acorn', женъ 'wives' (genitive plural) actually represented the sound *e*, and not, as in modern Russian, *o*. Subsequently, in specific circumstances varying in the different East Slavonic languages, in such words a *e* before a hard consonant came to be pronounced as *o*. This happened also [not only after the originally soft hush-sibilants, but after other soft consonants] in such cases as медъ 'honey', селъ 'villages' (genitive plural).[2] In the majority of cases the change in pronunciation was not recognised in the spelling, so that while the written forms remained желудь, жен, мед, сел, these words were pronounced жолудь, хон, м′од, с′ол. In the 18th century an attempt was made to introduce the symbol *iô* to represent this pronunciation (cf., for example, the title of the satirical journal *И то и сiô*) but met with no success. The symbol ё was used for the first time in print in 1797 by Karamzin, in his poem *Опытная*

---

[1] In the following table of possible combinations of consonant plus vowel in Old Russian according to Vinokur's simplified analysis, д represents the largest group of consonants (д, т, б, п, в, ф, м, з, с) which were hard in prehistoric times, but occurred before both front and non-front vowels; л represents the group л, р, н which could be soft even before а and у; к represents the velars к, г, х; and ш the group (hush-sibilants and ц) which were originally soft. [Ed.]

Front vowels					Non-front vowels						
д	де	дѣ	ди	дь	да	ду	до	ды	дъ	дя	—
л	ле	лѣ	ли	ль	ла	лу	ло	лы	лъ	ля	лю
к	—	—	—	—	ка	ку	ко	кы	къ	—	—
ш	ше	шѣ	ши	шь	ша	шю	—	—	—	—	—

[2] In Russian the change from *e* to *o* between a preceding soft and a following hard consonant took place regularly only where е (but not ѣ) was in a stressed position, e.g. сѣла but село́, жёлтый but желтѣть. [Ed.]

соломонóва мýдростъ published in the literary miscellany *Аони́ды*. The line 'Тамъ бѣ́дный пролива́етъ слёзы' is annotated: 'Бу́ква ё съ двумя́ тóчками на верьху́ замѣня́етъ iô'. Thus a letter to denote the sound *o* after a soft or originally soft consonant took its place in our alphabet. The fact that the use of this letter has not become regular is one of the greatest anomalies in the history of Russian spelling.

Old Russian differed from the contemporary language also in many of its grammatical forms. In the paradigms of the noun and the verb, for instance, there were three numbers instead of two: in addition to the singular and plural there was the dual, used in referring to two objects or their attributes. The forms of the dual were used in particular for pairs of objects, e.g. руцѣ́ 'hands', нозѣ́ 'feet', рука́ма и нога́ма 'with hands and feet' [instr.—as opposed to the plural forms ру́ци, нóзи, рука́ми и нога́ми]. The modern plurals óчи 'eyes', у́ши 'ears', плéчи 'shoulders', колéни 'knees', are relics of the dual number denoting parts of the body occurring in pairs.[1] In *Сказа́ние о Бори́се и Глéбе* Yaroslav the Wise invokes the memory of his two slain brothers in the words: О бра́та моя́! а́ще и тѣ́льмь ошьла́ еста́, нъ благода́тию жива́ еста́ и гóсподеви предъстóита и моли́твою помозѣ́та ми 'O my brothers, although you have departed in the body, by grace you are alive and stand before the Lord, help me with your prayers'. Here брата, ошьла, еста, жива, предъстоита and помозѣта are all dual forms.

In addition to the six cases of the modern language, Old Russian had a seventh, the vocative [used in addressing a person or thing]. In the same *Сказа́ние* we read in Gleb's prayer: Спаси́ ся ми́лыи мои óтьче и господи́не Васи́лие, спаси́ ся ма́ти и госпожé моя́, спа́си ся и ты бра́те Бори́се старѣ́ишино оу́ности моéя, спаси́ ся и ты бра́те и поспеши́тѣлю Я́рославе, спаси́ ся и ты бра́те и вра́же Святопъ́лче...'Be saved, my dear father and lord Vasiliy, be saved, my mother and lady, and be saved you my brother Boris, arbiter of my youth, and be saved you, my brother and helper Yaroslav, and be saved also you, my brother and enemy Svyatopolk'. Here all the words denoting persons apostrophised have the form of the vocative case. In modern Russian the words Бóже 'God' and Гóсподи 'Lord' are relics of this case.

[1] Cf. also the vulgar word for 'testicles' мудé, in which the original dual ending is preserved. [Ed.]

Originally there were more types of declension than in modern Russian. There were three declensions of masculine nouns, for instance. The word рабъ 'slave' was declined in the singular as follows:

Nom.	рабъ	Instr.	рабъмь
Acc.	рабъ or раба[1]	Prep.	рабѣ
Gen.	раба	Voc.	рабе
Dat.	рабу		

The word конь 'horse' belonged to the soft variant of the same ['*o-* stem'] declension:

Nom.	конь	Instr.	коньмь
Acc.	конь ог коня	Prep.	кони
Gen.	коня	Voc.	коню
Dat.	коню		

But the word волъ 'ox' was originally declined as follows ['*ŭ-* stem']:

Nom.	волъ	Instr.	волъмь
Acc.	волъ ог вола	Prep.	волу
Gen.	волу	Voc.	волу
Dat.	волови		

An example of the third ['*i-* stem'] declension is гусь 'goose':

Nom.	гусь	Instr.	гусьмь
Acc.	гусь	Prep.	гуси
Gen.	гуси	Voc.	гуси
Dat.	гуси		

The masculine noun путь is an isolated relic of this declension.

The corresponding differences in the plural may be illustrated by forms of рабъ and волъ:

Nom.	раби	волове
Acc.	рабы	волы
Gen.	рабъ	воловъ
Dat.	рабомъ	волъмъ
Instr.	рабы	волъми
Prep.	рабѣхъ	волъхъ

There was no vocative form in the plural or for neuter nouns.

[1] The use of the genitive form for the accusative case of masculine nouns denoting animate beings had already begun in the Old Russian period, but was not yet completely systematised, especially in the plural, in which these cases had different endings. [Ed.]

These declensions were subsequently amalgamated into one general type [e.g. modern стол], but numerous variant case forms have remained as relics. For example, in the genitive singular many masculine nouns may have either the ending -a or -у. Compare вы́воз табака́ 'the export of tobacco' and па́чка табаку́ 'a packet of tobacco'; одного́ ро́да 'of one kind' and без ро́ду, без пле́мени 'without kith or kin'; из тёмного ле́са 'out of a dark forest' and и́з лесу 'out of the forest', etc. Here the -у ending is the old genitive case ending of the волъ declension, retained in a specialised usage. Another example is the genitive plural, in which instead of the normal ending -ов derived from the волъ declension (e.g. столо́в, пиро́в, шаго́в) some nouns have a form identical with the nominative singular as in the рабъ declension, e.g. па́ра сапо́г 'a pair of boots', эскадро́н гуса́р 'a squadron of hussars', etc.

In modern Russian, gender differences in the plural case endings are negligible, but in Old Russian for example the endings of the dative, instrumental and prepositional differed greatly in various declensions, e.g.

Dat.	рабомъ	but	женамъ
Instr.	рабы	but	женами
Prep.	рабѣхъ	but	женахъ

Gradually the endings -ам, -ами, -ах supplanted the corresponding endings of all the other declensions, but even in the days of Peter I the old forms were no rarity, e.g. того́ ра́ди ко всѣмъ ку́рфірстомъ пи́сано 'so all the Kurfürsts were written to' (i.e. всем курфирстам), была́ конфере́нція съ депута́ты генера́ловъ статъ 'there was a conference with the deputies of the States General' (i.e. с депута́тами), о уготовле́ніи воины́ въ нідерла́ндѣхъ 'about the preparation for war in the Netherlands' (i.e. в Нидерла́ндах). These examples are taken from the newspaper *Ве́домости*, 1711. Here it is noteworthy that the archaic endings -омъ, -ы, -ѣхъ appear even in neologisms of Western origin. We see a relic of the old dative plural in the expression подело́м ему́ за э́то 'it serves him right', while isolated cases of the old instrumental plural occur in literature, e.g. in Pushkin's stylised lines in *Ска́зка о рыбаке́ и ры́бе*—за дубо́выми, тесо́выми воро́ты (instead of воро́тами), or in *До́мик в Коло́мне*—Hugo с това́рищи (instead of това́рищами).

The most important development in the adjective was the loss of the old nominal declension.[1] Such forms as добр, добра, добро, добры survive only in the nominative case and are now used exclusively in a predicative function. Relics of the original declension survive in such expressions as на босу́ но́гу 'without stockings', от мала́ до велика́ 'of all ages'.

An enormous difference exists between the forms of the Old Russian verb and that of modern Russian, especially in the past tense. Originally there were four separate sets of forms for the expression in various ways of a past action. The aorist (first singular идо́хъ 'I went', чита́хъ 'I read', моли́хъ 'I prayed') expressed an action which had occurred in the past, without reference to its completion or duration. Primarily the aorist was used in consecutive narration of events to state *what* had happened, by denoting the nature of the process itself. In the following quotation from the Laurentian copy of *Повесть временных лет* all the predicates are in the aorist: В лѣ́то 6479 при́де Святосла́въ в Переясла́вець, и затвори́шася Болга́ре в гра́дѣ. И излѣ́зоша Болга́ре на сѣ́чю про́тиву Святосла́ву и бысть сѣ́ча велика́.[1] 'In the year 6479 [i.e. A.D. 971, calculated from the supposed date of the Creation in 5508 B.C.] Svyatoslav came to Pereyaslavets and the Bulgarians shut themselves up in the town. And the Bulgarians came out to give battle to Svyatoslav, and there was a great battle.' However, the text continues: и одоля́ху Бълга́ре, which must be translated 'and the Bulgarians were winning'. The form одоля́ху is the second of the four past tenses, the imperfect (first person singular forms идя́ахъ or идя́хъ, чита́ахъ or чита́хъ, моля́ахъ or моля́хъ) which expressed a past action as a prolonged or repeated process. The third tense was a compound form called the perfect (e.g. шьлъ есмь 'I have gone', чита́лъ есмь 'I have read', моли́лъ есмь 'I have prayed') denoting a completed process having a result in the present. For example, under the year A.D. 6453 in the *Повесть* we read how Igor's retinue urged him to undertake further military ventures: О́троці Свѣньлъжи изодѣ́лися суть ору́жьемъ и порты́, а мы на́зи; поиди́, кня́же, с на́ми в дань, да и ты добу́деши и мы 'Sveneld's men are fitted out with arms and clothing, but we are naked. Prince, let us go out and gather tribute so that both you and we shall gain.' Here the perfect

[1] Originally adjectives declined as nouns of the *o-* and *a-* declensions. The modern forms are the result of the fusion of these 'short' forms with the third person pronoun и, я, е, etc., giving rise to compound forms, e.g. новъ+и became новый, нова+я > новая, нова+его > новаго. [Ed.]

изодѣлися суть must be translated as одѐты 'clothed', обзаведены́ 'provided with', i.e. Sveneld's men having completed a certain action in the past are now enjoying the result of this action. Thus пришьлъ есмь meant я нахожу́сь здесь 'I am here', and слыха́лъ есмь meant мне извѐстно, я зна́ю нѐчто, услы́шанное мно́ю 'I know something which I heard'. Finally, yet another compound tense, the pluperfect, existed to denote the location of an action in the distant past. This had two sets of forms: шьлъ бѣхъ or шьлъ былъ есмь 'I had gone', читалъ бѣхъ or читалъ былъ есмь 'I had read', молилъ бѣхъ or молилъ былъ есмь 'I had prayed', signifying the result of the completed process effective not in the present but in the past.

All these specific forms for the expression of these meanings were subsequently lost, and they are now rendered not by special forms of the verb, but by syntactical and stylistic means.[1] Of the four Old Russian tenses modern Russian has kept only the perfect, expressing the general meaning of past time. It has been simplified by the loss of the auxiliary verb есмь, еси́, есть, etc., leaving only the participial constituent of the compound form, so that instead of шьлъ есмь, читалъ есмь, молилъ есмь we now say simply шёл, чита́л, моли́л. It is because this form was originally a participle that, although it does not vary according to person, it alters according to gender and number—шла, шло, шли. One vestige of the old pluperfect is the folklore expression жи́ли-бы́ли 'Once upon a time there lived', derived from жили были суть with the loss of the auxiliary суть.

Finally we must mention one important feature of the Old Russian participles. In contrast with the modern language, the active participles could have both a nominal (short) form and a compound (full) form, e.g. сѣдя́ and сѣдя́и (cf. modern сидя́щий 'sitting'), сѣдѣвъ and сѣдѣ́выи (cf. modern сидѐвший).[2] The nominal form could be used as part of a compound predicate, e.g. есмь сѣдя 'I am sitting at the present moment', мужь бысть сѣдѣвъ 'the man was sitting at that moment', and also: пишу́ сѣдя 'I, being seated, am writing', мужь писа́ сѣдѣвъ 'the man, being at that time seated, wrote' (aorist). Later, in phrases like the latter two, the nominal participles

---

[1] And by the forms of the perfective and imperfective aspects. [Ed.]

[2] Cf. p. 6. All forms of these participles other than the nom. sing. masc. had the suffix -ч, e.g. fem. идучи, gen. sing. masc. идуча. It was from the compound forms of these cases (with the Church Slavonic suffix -щ replacing -ч) that the modern declinable participles were derived, e.g. идущи+я > идушая, идуща+его > идущего. [Ed.]

which originally, as participles, were syntactically related to the subject as a kind of predicative qualification of it, came to be understood as words relating to the *predicate*, i.e. as extensions of the predicate. This change in function was marked by the nominal forms of the active participles losing their flexions and becoming indeclinable gerunds [or verbal adverbs] e.g. пишу́, си́дя; написа́л, посиде́в, etc. Thus the modern gerunds are in origin the ancient nominal forms of the active participles.

It would be inappropriate here to launch into a more detailed description of the phonological and morphological structure of Old Russian, or the complexities of its development up till the present day. However, it must be emphasised that it is not at all difficult for a modern Russian speaker to understand Old Russian texts with relatively little preparation...

As an example let us take an extract from the Old Russian *Chronicle*, containing the legend of the death of Oleg, which is familiar to the Russian reader through the fine adaptation made by Pushkin (*Песнь о ве́щем Оле́ге*) who in turn took it from Karamzin's *Исто́рия госуда́рства росси́йского*. We quote the oldest extant text, preserved in a comparatively late copy of the *По́весть временны́х лет* in the 15th-century Königsberg or Radziwill manuscript. Here, and in all the examples that follow, slips of the pen have been corrected and the orthography and punctuation simplified:

И живя́ше Оле́гъ миръ име́а ко всемъ стра́намъ, княжа въ Ки́евѣ. И приспѣ́ о́сень. И помяну́ Оле́гъ конь свои, и́же бѣ поста́вилъ корми́ти, и не вседа́ти нань. Бѣ бо въпраша́лъ волхво́въ и куде́сникъ: отъ чего́ ми есть смерть? И рече́ ему́ куде́сникъ оди́нъ: Кня́же, конь его́же лю́биши и е́здиши на немъ, отъ того́ ти умре́ти. Оле́гъ же прии́мъ въ умѣ́ си рѣче́: Нико́ли же ся́ду нань, ни ви́жю его́ бо́ле того́. И повелѣ́ корми́ти и не води́ти его́ к нему́. И пребы́ нѣ́колико лѣтъ, не ви́дѣ его́, донде́же на гре́кы иде́. И пришле́дшу ему́ Кы́еву, и пребы́вьшю 4 лѣта, на пя́тое лѣто помяну́ конь, от него́же бя́хуть рекли́ волсви́ умре́ти. И призва́ старе́йшину ко́нюхомъ, рече́: Кде есть конь мъи, его́ же бѣ поста́вилъ корми́ти и блюсти́ его́. Он же рече́: у́мерлъ есть. Оле́гъ же посмеа́ся и укори́ куде́сника, река́: То ти непра́во глаго́лють вольсви́, но вся ложь есть, а конь у́мерлъ есть, а я живъ. И повелѣ́ оседла́ти конь, а то ви́жю ко́сти его́. И прии́де на мѣ́сто идѣ́ же бѣ́ша лежа́ще ко́сти его́ го́лы, и лобъ голъ. И ссѣ́де с коня́, и посмея́ся рече́: Отъ сего́ ли лба смьрть бы́ло взя́ти мнѣ? и въступи́ ного́ю на лобъ. И вы́никнувши змиа́ зо лба, укло́ну в но́гу, и с того́ разболѣ́ся и у́мре.

And Oleg lived ruling in Kiev and being at peace with all lands. Autumn came and Oleg remembered his horse which he had put out to grass, never to mount it [again]. For he had asked the wizards and magicians, 'How shall I die?' And one of the magicians said, 'Prince, that horse which you love and ride upon, from him you will die'. And Oleg noting this said, 'I shall never mount it nor see it again'. And he commanded that it should be fed and not brought to him. And several years passed and he did not see it, until that time when he went to fight the Greeks. And returning to Kiev and staying there for four years, in the fifth year he remembered the horse from which the wizards had said he would die. So he called the head groom and said, 'Where is my horse which I commanded to be fed and cared for?' He replied, 'It is dead'. Oleg laughed and rebuked the magician saying, 'So the wizards tell what is not true, it is false: the horse is dead and I am alive'. And he had his horse saddled—'I shall look at its bones'. And he came to the place where its bare bones were lying, and its bare skull, and got off his horse and said, laughing, 'Was it from this skull death was to take me?'—and he placed his foot on the skull. And a serpent darted out of the skull and bit his foot, and from that he fell ill and died.

It is unnecessary to explain the importance of the part played as an intermediary between Old Russian and the linguistic consciousness of the modern Russian reader, by the language of the Russian people and above all its folklore, in which so many phraseological and syntactical archaisms have been preserved.

4-2

6

THE RUSSIAN LITERARY LANGUAGE IN
THE EARLIEST PERIOD

Even the earliest monuments of Old Russian literature present us with a considerable wealth of varying styles. Corresponding to each of the three basic categories of texts (cf. p. 32) we can distinguish three basic types of written language: the bookish ecclesiastical style, the business style and the strictly literary style.

The two sources from which the Old Russian written language arose—the language of learning, with its roots in the Old Church Slavonic tradition, and the everyday language based on the living dialects of the Eastern Slavs—provided the substance for these styles, in which they were blended in various proportions. Naturally, neither of these sources remained static throughout the Old Russian period, and the stylistic functions of certain words and forms varied also. However, it is possible to define the general features of the three basic styles of language in relation to these sources.

The first style reveals an overwhelming predominance of the learned element, the colloquial element being present only as a slight admixture, introduced, on the whole, not intentionally, but involuntarily, for want of anything better. In the second [business style] on the contrary, the everyday element predominates and it is the learned element that stands out as a forced and artificial intrusion or borrowing. The most interesting is the third form, a linguistic blend in which the two elements enjoy more or less equal rights, so that in contrast to the other two, the language of the third type is intrinsically diverse and complex in style. Below we shall briefly illustrate and examine each of the three types.

The ecclesiastical-learned style is typical not only of the straight transcripts of Old Church Slavonic originals (usually in a Bulgarian version) but of all those works in Old Russian which are erudite and solemn in tone and which in their content and aims conform more or less to the ideology of the Orthodox Church. For obvious reasons, those translations [from Byzantine sources] which were carried out by Russians also belong to this category, it being natural that the translator would use the polished book language rather than the vernacular. Of the 11th-century texts written in this style special mention must be made of *Сло́во о зако́не и благода́ти* by the Metropolitan Ilarion, a sophisticated stylist and orator who had mastered all the refinements of Byzantine rhetoric and the art of 'weaving words' (изви́тие слове́с)[1] into an intricate pattern. Judging from later copies of the *Сло́во* Ilarion's Old Slavonic was impeccable (the earliest known text appears in a 16th-century copy). Ilarion confesses his devotion to the learned style in these words: Не къ невѣ́дущимъ бо пи́шемъ, но преизли́ха насы́щшемся сла́дости кни́жныя[2]—'For we write not for the untutored, but for those thoroughly steeped in the delight of books'. The following excerpt from *Сло́во о зако́не и благода́ти* illustrates this style of Old Russian:

Вся стра́ны, и гра́ды, и лю́діе чтутъ и сла́вятъ коего́ждо ихъ учи́теля, и́же научи́ша правосла́вной Вѣ́рѣ. Похва́лимъ же и мы, по си́лѣ на́шей, ма́лыми похвала́ми — вели́каа и ди́внаа сътво́ршаго на́шего учи́теля и наста́вника, вели́каго Кага́на на́шеа земля́, Влади́мера, вну́ка ста́раго И́горя, сы́на же сла́внаго Святосла́ва, и́же, въ своа́ лѣ́та влады́чьствующа, му́жствомъ же и хра́бърьствомъ прослу́ша въ страна́хъ мно́гахъ, и побѣ́дами и крѣ́постію помина́ются ны́нѣ и слову́тъ. Не въ худѣ́ бо и не въ невѣ́доми земли́ влады́-чьствоваша, но въ Ру́сской, я́же вѣ́дома и слы́шима есть всѣ́ми концы́ земля́...Добръ послу́хъ благовѣ́рію твоему́, о блаже́нниче, свята́а це́ркви Святы́а Богоро́дица Маріа, ю́же създа́ на правовѣ́рнѣй осно́вѣ, идѣ́же и му́жьственое твое́ тѣ́ло ны́нѣ лежи́тъ, ожыда́а трубы́ Арха́нгеловы. Добръ же зѣло́ и вѣ́ренъ послу́хъ сынъ твой Гео́ргій, его́жь створи́ Госпо́дь намѣ́стника по тебѣ́ твоему́ влады́честву, не руша́ща твои́хъ уста́въ, нъ утвержа́юща, ни умаля́юша твоему́ благовѣ́рію положе́ніа, но па́че прилага́юща, не казя́ща, нъ учиня́юща, и́же недоко́нчаннаа твоа́ доконча́, а́кы Соломо́нъ Давы́дова, и́же домъ Бо́жій вели́кый святы́й Его́ Прему́дрости създа́ на свя́тость и освяще́ніе гра́ду твоему́, ю́же съ вся́кою красото́ю украси́, зла́томъ и сребро́мъ и каме́ніемъ драгы́имъ, и съсу́ды че́стными, я́же це́ркви дивна и славна всѣ́мъ окру́гныимъ страна́мъ, я́коже ина не обря́щется въ всемъ полунощи земнѣ́мъ, отъ всто́ка дъ за́пада, и сла́вный градъ твой Кы́евъ вели́чьствомъ, я́ко вѣнце́мъ, обложи́лъ, пре́далъ лю́ди твоя́

---

[1] Like many other words, слово originally belonged to the 'consonantal' declension, with an extended stem in all cases except the nominative singular: genitive singular словесе, plural словеса́; cf. modern чу́до—pl. чудеса́, мать—gen. ма́тери, и́мя—gen. и́мени. [Ed.]

[2] This feminine genitive singular form of the adjective, which occurs very frequently until a much later period, is derived not from the Russian form новоѣ < новы+еѣ, but from Church Slavonic новыа. [Ed.]

и градъ Святѣй всеславнѣй, скорѣй на по́мощь Христіа́номъ, святѣй Бого-
ро́дици, е́йже и це́рковь на вели́кыихъ вратѣхъ създа́...Вста́ни, о че́стнаа
главо, отъ гро́ба твоего́, вста́ни, отряси́ сонъ! Нѣси́ бо у́мерлъ, но спи́ши
до о́бщаго всѣмъ вста́ніа. Вста́ни, нѣси́ у́мерлъ, нѣсть бо ти лѣ́по умрѣ́ти,
вѣ́ровавшу въ Христа́, живота́ всему́ мі́ру. Отряси́ сонъ, взведи́ о́чи...

All countries and cities and people honour and glorify each its own teacher who
taught it the true faith. Let us also in as far as we have strength praise with our
humble adulation our teacher and mentor who performed great and marvellous
deeds, the great Prince of our land Vladimir, the grandson of old Igor', the son
of glorious Svyatoslav, who reigning in their years by their manhood and valour
gained fame in many countries and are remembered and renowned to this day by
their victories and might. For it was not in a poor or an unknown land that they
reigned, but in the Russian land, which is known and renowned to all the ends of
the earth...A grand witness to your faith, o blessed one, is the holy church of the
Holy Virgin Mary which you set up on the foundation of true faith, where your
valiant body now lies awaiting the Archangel's trumpet. And also a most fine and
true witness is your son George [Yaroslav the Wise] whom the Lord has made
your successor after your Majesty, not breaking your laws but strengthening
them, not diminishing the fruits of your faith but adding to them, not destroying
but putting in good order, [and] who has completed what you left uncompleted,
as Solomon completed David's works, who to the blessedness and sanctity of your
city raised the great and sacred house of God, the temple of his wisdom [St Sophia],
which he has adorned with all manner of ornament, with gold and silver and
precious stones and with holy vessels, and this church is the marvel and glory of
all countries around, such that its like cannot be found in all the northern lands
from east to west, and has clothed your holy city of Kiev with majesty like a
crown, and has dedicated your people and your city to the Holy all-glorious
Mother of God, the speedy succour of Christians, and has built a church to her
at the great gate...Arise, O worthy leader, from your tomb, arise, cast off sleep!
For you are not dead, but sleep until all shall arise. Arise, you are not dead, you
cannot die, who believed in Christ the life of all the world. Cast off slumber, lift
up your eyes...

Other vivid examples of this style are found in the works of another
remarkable Old Russian orator, Kirill, Bishop of Turov, who lived
in the second half of the 12th century. His language and style can be
illustrated by the following extract from his *Сло́во въ но́вую недѣ́лю
по Па́сцѣ* (*Sermon for the first Sunday after Easter*):

Днесь весна́ красу́еться, оживля́юющи земно́е естьство́; бу́рніи вѣ́три, ти́хо
повѣва́юще, плоды́ гобьзу́ють и земля́ сѣмена́ пита́юще зеле́ную траву
ража́еть. Весна́ у́бо кра́сная вѣ́ра есть Христо́ва, я́же креще́ніемь поража́еть
человѣ́чьское пакые́ство; бу́рніи же вѣ́три грѣхотворе́ній по́мысли, и́же
покая́ніемь претво́ршеся на добродѣ́тель душеполѣ́зныя плоды́ гобьзу́ють:
земля́ же естьства́ на́шего, а́кы сѣмя Сло́во Бо́жіе прии́мши, и стра́хомь его́
при́сно боля́щи, духъ спасе́ніяража́еть. Ны́ня новоража́еми́ а́гньци и у́ньци,
бы́стро путь перу́ще, ска́чють, и ско́ро къ матеремъ възвраща́ющеся веселя́ть-
ся, да и па́стыри свиря́юще весе́ліемь Христа́ хва́лять. Агнеца, глаго́лю,
кро́ткыя отъ язы́къ лю́ди, а у́нца кумирослужи́теля невѣ́рныхъ странъ, и́же
Христо́вомь въчеловѣче́ніемь и Апосто́льскымь уче́ніемь и чюдесы́, ско́ро по

зако́нъ е́мъшеся, къ святѣ́й це́ркви възврати́вшеся, млѣ́ко уче́нія ссуть...
Ны́ня рата́и сло́ва, слове́сныя у́ньца къ духо́вному ярму́ приводя́ще, и
кре́стьное ра́ло въ мы́сленыхъ бразда́хъ погружа́юще, и бразду покаа́нія
почерта́юще, сѣ́мя духо́вное въсыпа́юще, надѣ́жами бу́дущихъ благъ
веселя́ться...

Today the Spring is resplendent, enlivening terrestrial Nature; the stormy winds
wafting gently make abundant the fruit, and the earth feeding the seeds brings
forth the green grass. The beautiful Spring is the faith of Christ which by baptism
causes the resurrection of men; and the stormy winds are sinful intentions which,
transformed by repentance into virtue, cause salutary fruits to flourish; and the
earth of our nature, welcoming the seeds of God's word and ever aching in fear of
it, brings forth the spirit of salvation. Today the newly born lambs and calves
gambol, swiftly tramping their path, and straightway returning to their mothers
they rejoice, while the shepherds playing on their pipes praise Christ with merri-
ment. The lambs I call the gentle people among the heathens, and the calves the
idolators of the infidel lands, who by the power of Christ's incarnation and the
teaching and miracles of the apostles having lately accepted the law, having
returned to the holy church, suck the milk of doctrine... Today the husbandmen
of the word, bringing the calves of the word to the spiritual yoke and sinking the
plough of baptism into the furrows of thought, tracing out the furrows of
repentance and scattering the seeds of the spirit, rejoice in the hope of blessings
to come...

(We must note in passing a curious feature of this allegorical style:
each allegory is commented on and explained immediately: Spring is
the Christian faith, the winds are sinful thoughts, the lambs are gentle
people among the heathens, etc.)

The style used for practical business, based as it was on everyday
usage, is diametrically opposed to the learned style. It occurs chiefly
in legal documents, particularly those which are concerned not with
solemn formalities, but with everyday matters. It has long been
recognised by historians of the Russian language that such documents provide the best material for the reconstruction of the living
Old Russian language. The most important early manuscript of this
kind is *Ру́сская пра́вда*, the analysis of which led S. P. Obnorsky
[1888–1962] to put forward for the first time the view that originally
the Russian written language was quite free from any Old Church
Slavonic influence. And in fact it is quite clear that, apart from the
script and the orthography, the link with the Church Slavonic
tradition is here so tenuous that it can be almost completely dis-
counted. However, we must bear in mind that the oldest Russian
texts are very varied in style, so that, as we have seen, other types of
language are possible. Here are some extracts from the oldest extant
copy of *Ру́сская пра́вда* (1282):

Оже при́деть кръва́въ моу́же на дворъ, и́ли синь, то видока́ емоу́ не иска́ти, нъ плати́ті емоу́ прода́жю 3 гри́вны. Или не боу́деть на немь знаме́ния, то привести́ емоу́ видо́къ, сло́во про́тивоу сло́ва, а кто боу́деть на́чалъ, томоу́ плати́ти 60 коунъ. Аче же и кръва́въ при́деть, и́ли боу́деть самъ поча́лъ, а вы́стоупять послоу́си, то то емоу́ за плате́жь, о́же и би́ли. Аже оуда́рить мече́мь а не оутнеть на смерть, то 3 гри́вны, а самомоу́ гри́вна за ра́ноу, о́же лѣче́бное. Потьнеть ли на смерть, то ви́ра. Или пьхне́ть моужь моу́жа лю́бо къ собѣ́, лю́бо от себе́, лю́бо по лицю́ оуда́рить, и́ли же́рдью оуда́рить а видока два вы́ведоуть, то 3 гри́вны прода́же.

Аже холо́пъ оуда́рить свобо́дна моу́жа, а оубѣжи́ть въ хоро́мъ, а господи́нъ его́ не вы́дасть, то плати́ти за нь господи́ноу 12 гри́внѣ, а за тѣмъ, а́че кдѣ налѣзѣть оуда́реныи тъ своего́ истьча́, кто же его оуда́рилъ, то Яросла́въ былъ оуста́вилъ и оуби́ти, нъ сынове́ его́ оуста́виша по отьци́ на коу́ны, лю́бо и би́ти розвяза́вше и́ли взя́ти гри́вна коунъ за соро́мъ.

Аже зажьже́ть гоумно́, то на пото́къ и на розграбе́жь домъ его́. Пе́реди па́гоубоу испла́тить а въ про́чи кня́зю поточи́ти и. Та́ко же о́же кто дворъ зажьже́ть. А кто па́кощами поре́жеть конь и́ли скоти́ноу, то прода́же 12 гри́вне а за па́гоубоу гри́вноу оуро́къ плати́ти.

If a man comes to the Prince's court bleeding or bruised, he need not seek a witness but is to be paid three grivnas as a fine. But if he bears no marks upon him then he must produce a witness [and confront his opponent] face to face, and he who started the fight must pay 60 kunas. But even if he appears bleeding, if it was he himself who started it and witnesses come forth, then he receives as payment [only] that he was beaten. If a man strikes [another] with a sword, but without killing him, then three grivnas, and one grivna to the [victim] himself for treatment of his wound. If he kills him then he [must pay] blood-money. If a man pulls or pushes another or strikes him in the face or strikes him with a staff, and two witnesses are produced, then he must pay a fine of three grivnas.

If a serf strikes a freeman and runs into the house, and his master will not give him up, then the master must pay twelve grivnas for him. And in the event that the man who was struck should encounter the man responsible for striking him, Yaroslav had established the right to kill him, but his [Yaroslav's] sons after their father's death decreed [instead] fines, either that he should be beaten, having been tied up, or that a fine of one grivna of kunas be taken for the offence.

If a man sets fire to a granary, then he is to be banished and his property confiscated. First the loss is to be made good and then the prince is to banish him. The same for anyone who sets fire to domestic buildings. And if anyone villainously kills a horse or a beast, then he must pay twelve grivnas and a levy of one grivna as compensation.

For comparison we quote below an extract from the treaty contracted by Prince Mstislav Davidovich of Smolensk with Riga and the 'Gothic shore' (the island of Gotland) in 1229. Its language bears clear traces of the dialect of Smolensk-Polotsk, and its stylistic features closely resemble those of *Ру́сская пра́вда*:

Кто бьеть дроу́га дѣ́ревьмь, а боу́дѣте синь лю́бо крова́въ, полоу́торы гри́вны серебра́ плати́ти емоу́. По оу́хоу оуда́рите 3 че́тврти серебра́. Послоу́ и попоу́ что оучи́нять, за дво́е того́ оузя́ти два платежя́. Аже кого́ оура́нять, полоу́торы гри́вны серебра́, а́же боу́дѣте без вѣка. Та́ко плати́ти оу Смолѣнеске и оу Ри́зе и на Го́чкомь берьзѣ.

If a man strikes another with a stick and causes bruising or bleeding, then he must pay one and a half silver grivnas. For striking on the ear three quarters of silver. If anything is done against an ambassador or a priest a double payment is to be taken. If a man is wounded, one and a half silver grivnas, if he is not maimed. So is it to be paid in Smolensk and Riga and on the Gothic shore.

The following late 13th-century marriage contract (складьство), between Teshata [the bride's father] and one Yakim, was drawn up in Pskov in the reign of Prince Dovmont (d. 1299):

Се поряди́ ся Тѣша́та съ Яки́момь про скла́дьство про пе́рвое и про за́дьнее. И на дѣвцѣ Яки́мъ серебро́ взялъ, а мони́ста Тѣша́тина у Яки́мовы женьı́ свобо́дна Тѣша́тѣ взя́ти. И роще́тъ оучини́ла проме́жи себе́, а бо́лѣ не на́добѣ Яки́му Тѣша́та, ни Тѣша́тѣ Яки́мъ. А на томь послоу́си Дави́дъ попъ Доро́жка, Домосла́въ Вѣко́шкынъ Боя́нъ, Кузма́ Лоико́вичь, Жиди́ло Жихно́вичь, Ива́нъ Смолня́нинъ. А кто си́и рядъ переступи́ть, Яки́мъ ли, Тѣша́та ли, тоть дасть 100 гри́венъ серебра́. А псалъ Довмо́нтовъ пи́сець.

Be it known that Teshata and Yakim have agreed on a marriage for present and future time. Yakim has received silver as a dowry, but Teshata retains the right to take back from Yakim's wife Teshata's jewellery. And they have settled accounts between them so that Teshata owes nothing more to Yakim, nor Yakim to Teshata. Witnesses to this are David Dorozhka priest [etc.] And if either break this agreement, whether Yakim or Teshata, he must pay 100 silver grivnas. Written by Dovmont's scribe.

The two types of written language illustrated so far manifest the uncompromising choice of one or other of two extremes. Somewhere between them lies the style which can be called the Old Russian literary language in the strictest sense of the word. As we have already pointed out, this style was created by the combination and interpenetration of the learned and the everyday language in such a way that, even if they did not yet actually fuse together to make a unified entity, they complemented each other, and at least the tendency towards such a fusion was there. The successive stages in the development of this synthesis can be observed, and it is important to fix the moment of its first appearance, even in embryo form. It will become clear below that this synthesis of the two sources of the language is the crux of the whole history of literary Russian, and it is above all in strictly literary works that it manifests itself in the earliest period.

The criteria of literary works as distinct from all others is that they were intended for *reading*, and not merely for some practical function such as historical records, legislation or liturgy. Among the reading-matter of Kievan Rus', apart from the most popular books of the Bible such as the Psalms (the function of which as popular reading was on the whole secondary), there exists quite a wide range of texts which can be called literary—works of a narrative, poetic or didactic nature. There are, for instance, descriptions of journeys, lives of the saints, homilies, poetical works such as *Слóво о полкý Йгореве*, the narrative parts of the *Chronicle* etc., which together constitute the nucleus of an indigenous Old Russian literature. There are also particular bonds between such works and the Old Russian folk epic. The following brief extracts from works of various types clearly demonstrate the nature of the Old Russian literary language as the unique product of the blending of two distinct elements.

Here is an extract from the *Testament* (*Поучéние*) of Vladimir Monomakh[1] which is preserved in the Laurentian copy of the *Chronicle*:

Тýра мя 2 метáла на розѣхъ и с конéмъ, олéнь мя одѝнъ болъ, а 2 лóси, одѝнъ ногáми топтáлъ, а другьɪ́й рогóма болъ, вепрь ми на бедрѣ мечь оття́лъ, медвѣдь ми у колѣна подъꙑклáда укусѝлъ, лю́тый звѣрь скочѝлъ ко мнѣ на бéдры и конь со мнóю повержé; и Богъ неврéжена мя съблюдé. И с коня́ мнóго падáхъ, гóлову си розбѝхъ двáжды, и руцѣ и нозѣ свои вередѝхъ, въ ýности своéй вередѝхъ, не блюдá животá своегó, ни щадя́ головьɪ́ своéя. Еже бьɪ́ло творѝти óтроку моемý, то самъ есмь сотворѝлъ, дѣлá на войнѣ и на лóвѣхъ, ночь и день, на знóю и на зимѣ, не дая́ собѣ упокóя; на посáдникы не зря, ні на биричи́, самъ творѝлъ, что бьɪ́ло нáдобѣ, весь наря́дъ, и в домý своéмь то я творѝлъ есмь; і в лóвчихъ лóвчий наря́дъ самъ есмь держáлъ и в кóнюсѣхъ, и о сóколѣхъ и о я́стрябѣхъ; то же и худáго смéрда и убóгьɪѣ вдовѝцѣ не далъ есмь сѝльнымъ обѝдѣти, и церкóвнаго наря́да и слýжбы самъ есмь призирáлъ. Да не зазрѝте ми, дѣти мои́, нъ инъ кто, прочéтъ, не хвалю́ бо ся ни дéрзости своéя, но хвалю́ Бóга и прославьля́ю мѝлость егó, и́же мя грѣ́шнаго и худáго селѝко лѣтъ сблюдъ отъ тѣхъ часъ смéртныхъ, и не лѣнѝва мя бьɪ́лъ сотворѝлъ, худáго, на вся дѣлá человѣ́чьская потрéбна. Да сю грáмотицю прочитáючи, потъснѣ́теся на вся дѣлá дóбрая, слáвяще Бóга с святьɪ́ми егó. Смéрти бо ся, дѣти, не бóйче ни рáти, ни отъ звѣ́ри но мужьскóе дѣло творѝте, кáко вы Богъ подáсть...

Twice I have been tossed with my horse on the horns of the aurochs, a reindeer has butted me, and two elks—one trampled me with its hooves and the other gored me with its antlers, a wild boar has torn the sword from my side, a bear has bitten the saddle-cloth at my knee, a wild beast has sprung at my loins and brought me down with my horse—and God has preserved me unharmed. And I have often fallen from my horse, twice cracked my skull, and I have hurt my

---

[1] Vladimir Vsevolodovich (1053–1125), Grand Prince of Kiev from 1113, was called after his maternal grandfather, the Byzantine Emperor Constantine Monomakhos. [Ed.]

arms and my legs in my youth, I have cared not for my life nor spared my head. Whatever my page had to do I did myself, in war and hunting, night and day, in heat and cold, giving myself no rest. Disregarding governors and heralds, I did myself all that was required, all administration, and in my house also I did this. I performed the huntsmen's tasks as a huntsman, and the stablemen's, and [looked after] the hawks and falcons. Nor did I allow the mighty to offend the defenceless peasant or poor widow, and I looked after the administration of the church and the service myself. Do not rebuke me, my children, or any other, reading this, for I do not praise myself or my prowess, but I praise God and glorify his mercy in preserving me, miserable sinner, for so many years from my hour of death, and in making me, worthless one, active in all that a man is required to do. When you read this document be filled with zeal for all good deeds, praising God and his saints. Fearing neither death nor battle nor wild beast, my children, do whatever manly tasks God sets you...

Next we quote a few lines from the 13th-century *Supplication of Daniil the Exile* (*Моле́ние Дани´ла За́точника*) from a copy which is unfortunately no earlier than the 16th century:

Лу́че бы ми ви́дети нога́ своя́ в лы́чницы в дому́ твое́мъ, не́жли в черле́нѣ сапозѣ в боя́рстемъ дворѣ́. Лу́че бы ми тобѣ́ в деру́зѣ служи́ти, не́жли в багряни́цы въ боя́рстемъ дворѣ́. Не лѣ́по бо усе́рязь злать в но́здри свíнíи, ни на холо́пехъ до́брыи портъ. Аще бы котлу́ золоты́ ко́льца во у́шию, но дну его́ не избы́ти че́рности, и жже́нíя его́, та́коже и холо́пу. Аще па́че мѣ́ры гордѣли́въ и буя́въ, но уко́ра ему́ своего́ не избы́ти холо́пия и́мени. Лу́че бы мí вода́ пи́ти в дому́ твое́мъ, не́жли пи́ти медъ в боя́рстемъ дворѣ́. Лу́че бы ми воробе́и испе́ченъ прíима́ти отъ руки́ твоея́, не́жли плеча́ бора́нья отъ руки́ злыхъ госуда́рь...Не мо́ре потопля́етъ кора́бль но вѣ́тры. Та́ко и ты кня́же не самъ впада́еши в печа́ль, но введу́тъ тя ду́мцы. Не огнь тво́ритъ ражже́нíе желѣ́зу, но надмѣ́нíе мѣшьно́е.

Уме́нъ мужь не вѣ́лми на ра́ти хоро́бръ быва́етъ, но крѣ́покъ въ за́мыслехъ...

It would be better for me to see my foot in a peasant's shoe in your house than in a scarlet boot at a boyar's court. It would be better for me to serve you in broadcloth than [serve] in purple at a boyar's court. For a gold earring is out of place in a swine's nostril, and costly apparel on slaves. If you were to put gold rings in the lugs of a cooking-pot you would not thereby get rid of the blackness and soot on its bottom—so it is with a slave. However proud and bold he be, he cannot escape being reproached with the name of a slave. It would be better for me to drink water in your house than to drink mead at a boyar's court. It would be better for me to take a baked sparrow from your hand than shoulder of mutton from the hand of wicked lords...It is not the sea that sinks a ship, but the winds. So it is not you yourself, prince, that fall into grief, but your counsellors who lead you there. It is not the fire that smelts iron, but the blowing of bellows.

A wise man may not be very valiant in battle, but he is firm in his intentions...

The following story from the Laurentian text of the *Primary Chronicle* under the year 992 is a model of the language and literature of the Old Russian period. It tells of a duel between a Russian warrior and a Pecheneg:

Literary language in the earliest period

И ста Володи́меръ на сей сторонѣ́, а Печенѣ́зи на о́ной, и не смя́ху си на о́ну страну́, ни они́ на сю страну́. И приѣ́ха князь Печенѣ́жьскый к рѣкѣ́, возва́ Володи́мера и рече́ ему́: «вы́пусти ты свой мужь, а я свой, да ся борета; да а́ще твой мужь уда́рить мои́мь, да не вою́емъ за три лѣ́та; а́ще намъ мужь уда́рить, да вою́емъ за три лѣ́та»; и разидо́стася ра́зно. Володи́меръ же при́де въ това́ры, и посла́ биричи́ по това́ромъ, глаго́ля: «нѣ́ту лі тако́го му́жа, и́же бы ся ялъ с Печенѣ́жиномь?» и не обрѣ́теся никдѣ́же. За́утра приѣ́хаша Печенѣ́зи и свой мужь приведо́ша, а у на́шихъ не бысть. И поча́ тужи́ти Володи́меръ, сля по всѣмъ во́емъ, и при́де еди́нъ старъ мужь ко кня́зю и рече́ ему́: «кня́же! есть у мене́ еди́нъ сынъ ме́ншей до́ма, а с четырми́ есмь вы́шелъ, а онъ до́ма, отъ дѣ́тьства бо его́ нѣсть кто имъ удари́лъ: еди́ною бо ми я сваря́щю, и о́ному мьня́щю усние, разгнѣ́вавься на мя, преторже́ че́реви рука́ма». Князь же се слы́шавъ ра́дъ бысть, и посла́ по нь, и приведо́ша и ко кня́зю, и князь повѣ́да ему́ вся; сей же рече́: «кня́же! Не вѣ́дѣ, могу́ ли со нь, и да иску́сять мя: нѣ́ту ли быка́ велика́ и силна́?» И налѣ́зоша быкъ вели́къ и силе́нъ, и повелѣ́ раздражди́ти быка́; возложи́ша на нь желѣ́за горяча́, и быка́ пусти́ша, и побѣ́же быкъ ми́мо и, и похвати́ быка́ руко́ю за бокъ, и вы́ня ко́жю с мя́сы, ели́ко ему́ рука́ зая́; и рече́ ему́ Володи́меръ: «мо́жеши ся с нимь боро́ти». И нау́трия придо́ша Печенѣ́зи, поча́ша зва́ти: «нѣ ли му́жа? се нашь доспѣ́лъ». Володи́меръ же повелѣ́ той но́щи облещи́ся в ору́жие, и приступи́ша ту обо́и. Вы́пустиша Печенѣ́зи мужь свои, бѣ бо превели́къ зѣло́ и стра́шенъ; и вы́ступи мужь Володи́мерь, и узрѣ́ и Печенѣ́зинъ и посмѣ́яся, бѣ бо сере́дний тѣ́ломь. И размѣ́ри́вше мѣ́жи обѣ́ма полко́ма, пусти́ша я къ собѣ́, и я́стася, и поча́ста ся крѣ́пко держа́ти, удави́ Печенѣ́зина въ рука́хъ до сме́рти, и удари́ имь о зе́млю; и кли́кнуша, и Печенѣ́зи побѣ́гоша, и Русь погна́ша по нихъ сѣку́ще, и прогна́ша я.

And Vladimir took up his stance on one side, and the Pechenegs on the other, and the former did not dare to cross to that side, nor the latter to this side. And the Pecheneg prince came to the river, called Vladimir and said to him: 'You send out your man and I shall send mine, and let them fight. And if your man vanquishes mine, then we shall make a truce for three years; but if it is our man who wins, then we shall wage war for three years.' They parted from each other. And Vladimir came to the encampment and sent his heralds around it saying, 'Is there no man who will take on the Pecheneg?', but nowhere was a man found. Next day the Pechenegs arrived with their man, and we had none. And Vladimir began to grieve, sending word to all his warriors. And one old man came to the prince and said to him: 'Prince, I have my youngest son at home. I came here with four others, but this one is at home. From his childhood there has never been anyone who could overcome him. For once when I rebuked him and he was stretching leather he became angry with me and tore the hide apart with his hands.' Hearing this the prince was glad and sent for him, and they brought him to the prince who told him about the affair. And he said, 'Prince, I know not whether I can overcome him, but let me be tested: do you have a great, strong bull?' And they found a great, strong bull and he told them to torment it. They touched it with a hot iron and let it out, and the bull ran past him and he caught it by the side with his hand and tore off skin and flesh, as much as his hand held. And Vladimir said to him, 'You can fight him.' And in the morning the Pechenegs came and started calling: 'Do you not have a man? See, ours is ready.' Vladimir had ordered his man at night to put on armour, and they both came forth. The Pechenegs sent out their man, and he was gigantic and fearsome, and when

Vladimir's man came out the Pecheneg saw him and laughed, for he was of medium build. And having measured out lists between the two armies they set them upon each other, and they grappled and gripped each other tightly, and he strangled the Pecheneg with his hands and threw him down on the ground. A cry went up and the Pechenegs fled, and the Russians gave chase, smiting them, and scattered them.

What then constitutes the basis of the stylistic differences which we immediately sense when we compare examples of the three types of literature? These differences appear in every aspect of the language, but involve primarily vocabulary and syntax.

It is easy to appreciate, in the first place, the stylistic significance of lexical variants based on phonetic differences, that is to say, parallel forms of the same word which arose in prehistoric times as a result of the different phonological developments of the Bulgarian dialects on the one hand, and the Eastern Slavonic dialects on the other. This resulted in such doublets as градъ—гóродъ 'town', свѣштá—свѣчá 'candle', надéжда—надéжа 'hope', etc. Words such as градъ, главá, etc. could be completely assimilated into literary usage because their form was not at variance with the Eastern Slavonic sound system: as Russian already contained a certain number of words in which the combinations -ра- and -ла- occurred between two consonants, e.g. травá, плáвать, such words as градъ and главá easily found a place in the language alongside the vernacular гóродъ and головá. These lexical doublets, however, were not absolutely identical, but differed either stylistically or semantically. The choice between градъ and гóродъ, for example, depended on the fact that градъ had a learned connotation while гóродъ was colloquial or simply neutral so far as style was concerned. This is why in the extracts cited from Ilarion and Kirill Turovsky we find only стрáны, грáды, владыʹчьствующа, хрáбърьствомъ, злáтомъ, драгыʹимъ, вратѣхъ, главо (vocative), възвращáющеся, млéко, браздáхъ, etc., without a single occurrence of the Russian [полногласие] pattern -оро-, -оло-, -ере- between consonants (cf. p. 8). Conversely, in the extracts from legal documents we find only the Russian forms холóпъ (cf. Church Slavonic хлап, the name for knave in the old card-playing terminology), хорóмъ, сорóмъ, пéреди, дѣревъмь, о бéрьзѣ (i.e. о бéреге), etc.

In truly literary texts, however, we immediately find the parallel usage of words with either form. Thus in Vladimir Monomakh's *Поучéние*, неврéжена occurs along with вередúхъ, in Daniil the

61

Exile's *Моле́ние* we find both усеря́зъ златъ and золоты́ ко́льца, in the *Chronicle* story of the duel between the Russian and the Pecheneg both на сей стороне́ and на одну́ страну́, на сю страну́. It might appear that the choice between possible variants was a matter of mere chance, as if the writer was completely indifferent whether he wrote зла́то or зо́лото, страна́ or сторона́. Indeed it is very difficult to understand why in *Сло́во о полку́ И́гореве* we find Яросла́вна ра́но пла́четь Пути́влю го́роду на заборо́лѣ, 'Yaroslavna laments in the early morning on the ramparts of the city of Putivl'', and a few lines below in an exactly analogous place: Яросла́вна ра́но пла́четь въ Пути́влѣ на забра́лѣ. The most interesting thing is that this indifference apparently conforms to some law of its own. Thus in the translation of Josephus' *History of the Jewish War*, within the space of two pages we find first раставля́я съсоу́ды ра́тныя по забра́ломъ 'mounting the war vessels along the ramparts', and then и ста́вше по заборо́ломъ огнь мета́ху 'and standing on the ramparts they cast fire'. In the Hypatian copy of the *Chronicle* we find the same variety: in one place бысть ра́нено стоя́щихъ на забра́лѣхъ сто и шестьдеся́тъ 'one hundred and sixty of those standing on the ramparts were wounded', and in another взлѣзше на заборо́ла 'climbing on to the ramparts'.

There is no doubt that in a large number of such cases pure chance operates, so that the only useful lesson to draw is that Old Russian writers did not consider it reprehensible to have such a mixed vocabulary, and certainly did not feel obliged to avoid it. We cannot stop there, however: in the earliest texts we can frequently observe the conscious choice of one form in preference to the other, in dependence upon specific considerations of style. Thus, in the Laurentian copy of *По́весть временны́х лет* we read Оле́г нача́ го́роды ста́вити 'Oleg began to build towns' [specific and prosaic], but a little later, in the story of the conquest of Kiev, Oleg says: Се бу́ди ма́ти градо́мъ ру́сьскимъ 'Let this be the mother of Russian cities' [a solemn, rhetorical phrase]. In the account of the taking of Korsun' we read Посла́ Володи́меръ ко царе́ма Васи́лью и Костянти́ну, глаго́ля си́це: Се градъ ва́ю сла́вный взяхъ 'Vladimir sent to the Emperors Basil and Constantine, saying, 'Behold I have captured your [genitive dual pronoun] famous city'. Here it seems quite possible that градъ is used in an ironic sense. If this is so, then it is one of the earliest cases of the ironic usage of Slavonicisms in

Russian (which was to become so common in the 19th and 20th centuries). We find the [native Russian] word вóрогъ in the sentence Тъ есть вóрогъ нáма и Рýсьстѣи земли́ 'This is the enemy of us [dual] and of Russia', but the stylistic [solemn] use of the [Church Slavonic] variant врагъ is understandable in the phrase я́ко Госпóдь избáвилъ ны есть отъ врагъ нáшихъ, и покори́ врáгы нáша 'As the Lord hath delivered us from our enemies and subdued our enemies'. Directly after this we read: и скруши́ глáвы змиéвыя 'and crushed their serpents' heads', but the use of the vernacular form is understandable in reporting the grumbling of the retinue: зло есть нáшимъ головáмъ, да намъ я́сти деревя́ными лъжи́цами, а не срéбряными 'we are unfortunate that we have to eat with wooden spoons and not with silver ones'. In the account of the calling in of the Varangians we read Поидѣте... володѣти нáми 'come to rule over us', whereas Vladimir Monomakh in his *Поучéние* has the ready-made ecclesiastical formula Госпóдь нашь, владѣя животóмъ и смéртью 'Our Lord, ruling our life and our death'. The Church Slavonic variant чрéво is preserved in the Biblical quotation изъ чрéва прéже денни́ца роди́хъ тя 'I gave birth to you from my belly before dawn', whereas the heroic warrior Budy provokes the Polish king Boleslav to battle in the words: Да то ти пробóдемъ трѣскóю черéво твоé тóлъстое 'Sure we will pierce your fat belly with a staff'.

Under certain conditions this stylistic choice between the Russian and Old Church Slavonic variants gradually becomes overlaid by a real semantic differentiation. For example, храмъ is used almost exclusively in the meaning 'God's house, church', whereas хорóмъ means 'a house' in general, e.g. а пристáвимъ вы хорóмовъ руби́ти нáшихъ 'we shall make you build our houses'. According to the context, a hostile person may be described as either врагъ or вóрогъ, but in the meaning 'the devil', the arch-enemy of mankind, only врагъ is used. In the *Chronicle* the cry emitted by Yaropolk as he is treacherously murdered (*c.* 1086) is Охъ, тотъ мя врáже улови́ 'Ah, devil, you have caught me', with врáже [vocative] used metaphorically of the murderer. This tendency gave rise to purely semantic oppositions of words, e.g. храни́ти 'preserve'—хорони́ти 'bury', власть 'power'—вóлость 'province', etc., which have been current in Russian ever since the Middle Ages, mainly in literature. Admittedly one still finds in *Пóвесть временны́х лет*, on the one hand похорони́ вóи в лóдьях 'he hid his soldiers in the boats', and on the other схрани́ша тѣ́ло его́ 'they buried his body' [i.e. the converse of the distinction mentioned above], but this is rare, and on the whole these verbs are differentiated in the same way as in modern Russian. Finally, in certain cases only one of the potential pair of forms occurs, the second form either having become obsolete very quickly, or perhaps in fact never having existed in the Eastern Slavonic or Bulgarian vernaculars. Thus, for example, the words влады́ка 'master', блаже́нъ 'blessed', огласи́ти 'publish', сла́дъкъ 'sweet', зракъ 'pupil' on the whole do not have parallel Russian forms, while conversely Church Slavonic forms occur scarcely, if at all, for the Russian во́локъ 'portage', коло́да 'block of wood', соро́чька 'shirt', узоро́чье 'costly raiment', скоморо́хъ 'minstrel'.

What has been said above about such doublets as градъ—го́родъ can also be applied in other cases (of which there is a large number) in which the co-existence of the Russian and Church Slavonic sources of the written language resulted in the existence of parallel means of expression. Among these are many synonyms, such as пра́вьда, the colloquial Russian word for 'truth', and и́стина, the Church Slavonic word. Similarly [with the Russian form always quoted first] щека́—лани́та 'cheek', лъбъ—чело́ 'forehead', грудь—пьрси 'breast', ши́я—вы́я 'neck', гу́бы—у́стьны (usually in the dual form устьнѣ) 'lips', плугъ (a Germanism)—ра́ло 'plough', ... пло́тьникъ—дрѣводѣлъ 'carpenter', and many others. The stylistic difference in such pairs of words is borne out by the types of context in which they are used. For example, Kirill of Turov uses the Church Slavonic ра́ло in the symbolic expression крьстное ра́ло въ мы́сленыхъ бразда́хъ погружа́юще 'sinking the plough of the cross in the furrows of the mind', whereas in legal documents the colloquial word плугъ is used in the Old Russian expression for a measure of area: куда́ плугъ ходи́лъ 'where the plough has passed'.

The blending of the language of everyday speech and that of learning also produced a great variety of homonyms. Thus, for instance, the word живо́тъ in everyday speech meant 'belongings' (иму́щество, пожи́тки), e.g. in the *Novgorod Primary Chronicle*: о́вы огне́мъ погорѣ́ша въ дворѣ́хъ надъ животы́ 'some were burned in their homes over their belongings', but in the literary language it meant 'life', as for instance in the same text: Ста́ти всѣ́мъ лю́бо живо́тъ, лю́бо смерть за пра́вду новгоро́дскую 'All must stand in life or death for the laws of Novgorod', or in Vladimir Monomakh:

не блюдá животá своегó 'not taking care for my life'. Compare also the still current expression борьбá не на живóт, а на смерть 'a life and death struggle'. The word буи (cf. modern Russian бýйный 'wild') in the vernacular meant 'bold, valiant', but in the learned style 'foolish, vain, sinful'. Compare on the one hand its use in *Слóво о полкý Ѝгореве*: Рáны Ѝгоря, бýего Святъслáвлича 'the wounds of valiant Igor′ Svyatoslavich', and on the other the nuance of censure in Kirill of Turov's sermon: бýе слóво 'foolish word'. Similarly, in the words of Daniil the Exile пáче мѣры гордѣлѝвъ и буѧвъ 'excessively arrogant and headstrong', and in Vladimir Monomakh's supplication to the Virgin Mary: отимѝ отъ убóгаго сéрдца моегó гóрдость и бýесть 'take from my poor heart pride and vanity'. Colloquially, цѣловáти meant 'to kiss', as in modern Russian (cf. the bookish equivalent лобъзáти) but in the ecclesiastical language it meant 'to greet, welcome', e.g. in *Пóвесть временнѝх лет*: Прѝде в Печéрьскый монастѝрь и брáтья цѣᴫ вáша и съ рáдостью 'He came to the Monastery of the Caves, and the brothers greeted him with joy'. Further examples of homonyms are [the Russian meaning always preceding that in Church Slavonic]: страдáти 'to work' and 'to suffer', лáяти 'to bark' and 'to lie in ambush for', вьрстá 'verst' and 'age', пѝво 'beer' and 'beverage' in general, сѣно 'hay' and 'grass' in general, etc.

The syntax of the Old Russian literary language also reveals the combination of two inherently different linguistic structures: the oral, with its characteristically loose linking of the parts of an utterance, and the learned, in which the flow of language fits harmoniously into a planned syntactical pattern. Old Russian tends to reveal, under a polished exterior, colloquial turns of phrase with their directness and their own peculiar 'disorder' (несклáдица), their chaotic arrangement of words, their preference for constructions composed of coordinated principal clauses [parataxis] rather than subordinative constructions in which the combination of clauses creates an indivisible entity [hypotaxis]—in short, with their absence of what Potebnya[1] very aptly called 'syntactical perspective'. Consider, for example, the following passage from the *Primary Chronicle* describing the route 'from the Varangians to the Greeks':

Полянómъ же жѝвшимъ осóбѣ по горáмъ симъ, бѣ путь изъ Варя́гъ въ Грéки и изъ Грекъ по Днѣпрý, и верхъ Днѣпрá вóлокъ до Лóвоти, и по

---

[1] A. A. Potebnya (1835–91), an outstanding Russian philologist. [Ed.]

Лѣвоти внити въ Илмѣрь о́зеро вели́кое, из него́же о́зера потечѐть Во́лховъ и въ течѐть в о́зеро вели́кое Нево́, и того́ о́зера вни́деть у́стье в мо́ре Варя́жьское, и по тому́ мо́рю ити́ до Ри́ма, а отъ Ри́ма прити́ по тому́ же мо́рю ко Царюго́роду, а от Царяго́рода прити́ въ Понтъ мо́ре, въ нѐже втечѐть Днѣпръ рѣка́.

The Polyane living apart on these hills, there was a route from the Varangians to the Greeks along the Dnepr, and at the head of the Dnepr a portage to the Lovat', and by the Lovat' to go to the great lake Il'men' from which lake flows the Volkhov and flows into the great lake Nevo, and the mouth of this lake enters the Varangian sea, and by that sea to go to Rome, and from Rome by that same sea to come to Constantinople, and from Constantinople to come to the Black Sea into which flows the river Dnepr.

A little further on the opinion that the founder of Kiev was a simple ferryman is refuted in the following words:

Аще бо бы перево́зникъ Кий, то не бы ходи́лъ Царюго́роду; но се Кий княжа́ше в ро́дѣ своѐмь; и приходи́вшю ему́ ко царю́, я́коже сказа́ють, я́ко вели́ку честь прия́лъ отъ царя́, при кото́ромъ приходи́въ цари́.

For if Kiy was a ferryman then he would not have gone to Constantinople; but behold Kiy was reigning in his tribe, and arriving at the Emperor, as they say, that he received great honour from the Emperor, in the reign of which Emperor he came.

The absence of the logically articulated sentence structure to which literate people are nowadays so used, often gives the reader the impression of jumping from one idea to another, or that extraneous remarks are constantly intruding into the narrative, e.g. И стоя́ше Володи́меръ обры́вся на Дорогожи́чи, мѐжи Дорогожи́чемъ и Ка́пичемъ, и есть ровъ и до сего́ дне 'And Vladimir stood entrenched at Dorogozhich, between Dorogozhich and Kapich, and there is a ditch there to the present day'; or, from the *Testament* of Vladimir Monomakh: Пѐрвое к Росто́ву идо́хъ, сквозѣ Вя́тичѣ, посла́ мя отѐць, а самъ и́де Ку́рьску 'First I came to Rostov by way of the Vyatichi, my father sent me, while he himself went to Kursk'. In Old Russian there was no such thing as 'indirect speech', but only direct, the quoted words frequently being tacked on to the preceding phrase without any warning, as, for instance, in the legend of Oleg's death quoted above: И повелѣ́ осѣдла́ти конь, а то ви́жю ко́сти его́ 'And he had his horse saddled—"I shall look at its bones"'. On the other hand we sometimes find direct speech introduced by a conjunction as if it were indirect speech, e.g. И присла́ въ Но́вгородъ, я́ко не хоцю́ у васъ княжи́ти 'And he sent word to Novgorod that "I do not want to be your prince"' (*Primary*

Chronicle). These are constructions which subsequently occur in uneducated, semi-literate speech, e.g. in Gogol's *Ревизо́р*: Вот тепе́рь тракти́рщик сказа́л, что не дам вам есть, пока́ не заплати́те за пре́жнее 'The innkeeper said just now that "I shan't give you anything to eat until you pay for what you've had already"' The extent of this primitive tendency to loose sentence construction is indicated by such phrases as: поста́вилъ це́рковь свята́го Нико́лу (instead of Нико́лы) 'built the church of/to Saint [genitive] Nikola [accusative]'; or кто мо́жетъ послу́ словеса́мъ его́ отвѣ́тъ дать (instead of словеса́мъ посла́) 'who can give an answer to the ambassador to his words'—where two independent cases have been used in parallel instead of the modern integrated case structure. Such manifestations of parataxis, embedded in the literary syntax derived from Byzantine literature, give the Old Russian literary language its own peculiar flavour.

Other constructions typical of the Old Russian literary language include certain features borrowed from Greek, such as the substantival use of adjectives in the neuter plural rather than the singular, e.g. потре́бьная имъ дая́хъ, i.e. дава́л им ну́жное 'I gave them what was necessary'. Another very frequent feature of Old Russian literary syntax which is totally unknown in the vernacular is the 'dative absolute' construction [of a noun or pronoun with a participle] known in Russian as да́тельный самостоя́тельный. For example, we read in the legend of the death of Oleg: И пришéдшу ему́ Кы́еву..., i.e. И когда́ он пришёл в Ки́ев...'And coming to Kiev...' or 'And when he came to Kiev'. On the other hand the 'nominative absolute' construction was typical of colloquial Russian, e.g. а вы плóтници су́ще, а приста́вимъ вы хорóмовъ руби́ти на́шихъ 'as you are carpenters we shall make you build houses for us' [су́ще is the present participle of бы́ти, cf. modern бу́дучи].

67　　　　5-2

7

THE LITERARY LANGUAGE IN THE
15TH–17TH CENTURIES

In the latter part of the Russian Middle Ages, in the cultural environment of the expanding and flourishing Muscovite state, the stylistic relationships described above underwent important changes.

It is obvious that the culture of Muscovy owed a great deal to that of Kievan Rus', and that the written language developed in the earliest period of Russian literature is one of the most significant parts of this legacy. In the preceding chapter we saw that one of the elements that went to make up this language was the living Eastern Slavonic language in its various dialects. During the period between the emergence of Russian literature and the rise of Moscow many changes had taken place in these dialects. Moreover, by the period now under consideration the three main groups of Eastern Slavonic dialects had established themselves, namely Russian, Ukrainian and Belorussian. Naturally it was the Russian vernacular which provided the basis to which the traditional written language had to be adapted in order to become the means of expression of the new political and cultural entity of Muscovy. As a result, many elements which had originally entered the written language with colloquial or at least stylistically neutral status, were already felt to be 'bookish' in 15th- and 16th-century Moscow. For example, in the 10th century the same [palatalised] form of the dative singular in the -a declension was common to the vernacular and the literary languages of Eastern Slavdom, e.g. рука́—руцѣ, нога́—нозѣ. By the 15th century, however, these archaic forms were already disappearing from living speech in the central provinces of Muscovy, and being superseded by the forms рукѣ and ногѣ. In the literary language, however, these archaic forms were still possible and indeed frequently obligatory. Thus what had once been a colloquial or neutral feature of the written now acquired the character of a learned element. It seems clear then that the literary language inherited from Kievan Rus′ must have sounded generally more 'learned' to cultured people in Muscovy than it had done to those who originally created it.

The written language of the 15th to 17th centuries contained quite a number of such categories newly endowed with a bookish flavour—for example, the dual number, the vocative case, the aorist and imperfect tenses, and various other forms which had become archaisms known to literate Muscovites only from books. Furthermore, such people had almost completely lost the distinction between those elements in the learned language which had been borrowed from the Church Slavonic source (e.g. градъ, нощь) and archaic words and forms formerly current in colloquial Russian itself (e.g. руцѣ, ногáма). Elements of both types were stylistically identical, all equally felt to be elements of the learned, ecclesiastical language, which was quite distinct from that of everyday intercourse. Thus from the 15th century onwards such elements as градъ, нощь, руцѣ, ногáма, etc., irrespective of their actual origin, were all considered to be Slavonicisms. The number of Slavonicisms in this sense was destined to increase as various elements of Old Russian became obsolete but lingered on in literary usage. By the beginning of the 18th century, for instance, the dative plural form столóмъ had become a 'Slavonicism', because in everyday speech the form used was столáм.

Slavonicisms of a kind existed in pronunciation also. If, because of natural phonological developments, noticeable contradictions have arisen between the spelling of a language and its pronunciation, then there will be a tendency for literate people to pronounce words not as they are in the vernacular, but as they are written—'по бýквам'. At certain periods in the development of a written language the aura surrounding it, as the language of the literate and learned, makes people feel that such a 'spelling-pronunciation' is correct and exemplary. A somewhat similar situation is that of the modern schoolchild making progress in learning to read, who begins to pronounce его as [jego] instead of [jevo]. In the Muscovite era there existed a school of thought which insisted that learned pronunciation should be based on a literal reading of the individual letters. For instance, they tried to pronounce the letter e always as an *e*, even where it was consistently pronounced as *o* in ordinary speech, e.g. in such words as женъ and медъ (cf. p. 44). This is the reason for the preservation in modern Russian of many words in which the vowel *o* (ё) ought to appear instead of *e* [because stress falls on the syllable in question], but in which nevertheless *e* occurs. Compare, for example, нéбо 'sky' and the dialect form нёбо (the same form appears in standard Russian with the meaning 'palate'), крест 'cross' and крéстный отéц 'godfather', вселéнная 'universe' and вселённый 'installed, lodged', etc. All these are Slavonicisms of pronunciation which survive as relics in the contemporary language, but were formerly obligatory in the appropriate style of speech. Further phenomena of this kind include the retention of óканье in the elevated style long after áканье had been established as the norm in the everyday speech of the capital,[1] and the attempt to maintain a difference between ѣ and e, although this had finally disappeared from Moscow pronunciation probably at some time in the 17th century. Finally, another characteristic of learned pronunciation was the pronunciation of the letter г as the voiced fricative [ɣ] instead of the plosive [g]. The fricative [which is normal in Ukrainian] came into the learned tradition from Southern Russia, the original cradle of the learned language. In the 18th century this pronunciation of г was still considered correct at least in certain words. For instance, in Peter the Great's reign the writer Pososhkov[2] wrote хрѣхъ instead of грѣхъ 'sin', obviously indicating that the initial consonant was to be pronounced as [ɣ]. This tradition is still apparent in modern Russian in the pronunciation of Бог as [boɣ], and occasionally ['blaɣo, ba'ɣatəj], etc. for блáго, богáтый.

The period of the so-called 'second South Slavonic influence', beginning at the end of the 14th century, was of the utmost importance in the history of the written language. This term covers certain characteristic developments arising from the conquest of southeastern Europe by the Turks, when the main centre of Orthodox culture shifted from the Balkans to Moscow.[3] Before this there had

---

[1] So that, for instance, дорогой would be pronounced not as [dəra'goj] but as [doro'goj]. [Ed.]

[2] I. T. Pososhkov (1652–1726), author of *Кнѝга о скýдости и богáтстве*, one of the first Russian books on economics. [Ed.]

[3] The Ottoman Turks crossed the Dardanelles to Gallipoli in 1355 and by 1400 had overrun Bulgaria and Serbia. Orthodox culture in the Balkans was finally stifled by the conquest of Constantinople in 1453. One result of this was a considerable exodus of scholars from these countries, many of them taking up residence in Kiev and other parts of Russia. [Ed.]

been a period of intense literary activity among the Balkan Slavs, which was characterised, among other things, by an archaising and decadent trend inspired by Byzantine models. In the 14th–15th centuries emigrants from the Balkan countries brought this love of archaism and stylistic affectation to Moscow, and a rash of archaisms and Bulgarisms appeared in Russian orthography. The 'big *yus*' (ѫ) was reintroduced—according to a characteristic confession of the scholars of the time 'for ornament and not for truth' (красоты́ ра́ди, а не и́стинно); iotated *a* [modern я] was avoided, so that they would write копіа, всеа, возглашаа instead of ко́пія 'spears', всея́ 'all' [genitive singular feminine], возглаша́я 'proclaiming'; ъ and ь were confused; and in imitation of Old Church Slavonic such spellings as плъкы, врьху were adopted instead of полкы 'regiments' and верху 'top'. On the whole this orthography proved to be a transient fashion, and it was on the vocabulary, phraseology and syntax of literary Russian that the second South Slavonic influence left a more definite mark.

This influence was also responsible for the exotic flowering of the 'weaving of words' (изви́тие слове́с or плете́ние слове́с) which some authors particularly prided themselves on. For instance, Yepifaniy the Wise[1] writing in the 15th century in his *Life of St Stephen of Perm'* (*Житие́ Стефа́на Пе́рмского*) says of himself:

Но доко́лѣ не оста́ну мно́го глаго́лати, доко́лѣ не оста́влю похвале́нію слова́, доко́лѣ не преста́ну предло́женаго и продлъжнаго хвалосло́вія? Аще бо и мно́гажды въсхотѣ́лъ быхъ изъоста́вити бесѣ́ду, но обаче любы́ его влече́тъ мя на похвале́ніе и на плете́ніе слове́съ.

But how long shall I not cease to speak abundantly, how long shall I not forsake words of praise, how long shall I not desist from ornate and loquacious rhetoric? Although I may often have wished to stop talking, still my love for it draws me on to eulogy and the weaving of words.

And here are some samples of his eulogies (хвалосло́вія) motivated by the author's admiration for the hero of his narrative:

Коль мно́го лѣтъ мно́зи фило́софи елли́нстіи събира́ли и соста́вливали гра́моту гре́ческую и едва́ уста́вили мнозѣ́ми труды́ и мно́гыми вре́мены едва́ сложи́ли; пе́рьмскую же гра́моту еди́нъ чрьнѐцъ сложи́лъ, еди́нъ соста́вилъ, еди́нъ счини́лъ, еди́нъ калоге́ръ, еди́нъ мнихъ, еди́нъ и́нокъ, Стефа́нъ глаго́лю, присноспомнимый епи́скопъ, еди́нъ въ еди́но вре́мя, а не по мно́га вре́мени и лѣта, я́коже и они́, но еди́нъ и́нокъ, еди́нъ вьединѐный и уединя́ася, еди́нъ, уединѐный, еди́нъ у еди́ного бо́га по́мощи прося́, еди́нъ

[1] A monk of the Trinity monastery (subsequently called Тро́ице-Се́ргиева ла́вра) at Zagorsk. [Ed.]

71

Literary language in the 15th–17th centuries

еди́ного бо́га на по́мощь призыва́а, еді́нъ еди́ному бо́гу моля́ся и глаго́ля: «бо́же и го́чподи, и́же прему́дрости наста́вниче и смыслуда́вче, несмы́с-ленымъ каза́телю и ни́щимъ засту́пниче: утверди́ и вразуми́ се́рдце мое́ и дай же ми сло́во, о́тчее сло́во, да тя прославля́ю въ вѣ́кы вѣко́мъ.

How many years did many Greek philosophers spend in compiling and collating the grammar of Greek, and [yet] by dint of many labours they hardly succeeded in establishing it and after much time scarcely could compose it. But one monk it was who composed the writing of the language of Perm', one man compiled it, one monk, one cenobite, one brother, I mean Stephen the most memorable Bishop, alone in one space of time and not, like them, after much time and years, but a lone cenobite, sequestered alone and withdrawn, one man, solitary, alone, asking the only God for help, alone calling upon the only God for his aid, alone praying to the only God and saying, 'O God and Lord, thou preceptor of wisdom and mentor, guide to the ignorant and protector of the poor, strengthen and make wise my heart and give me the word, the word of the Father, so that I may praise Thee for ever and ever.'

In another passage we read:

Тебе́ же, о епи́скопе Стефа́не, Пе́рмскаа земля́ хва́литъ и чтить я́ко апо́стола, я́ко учи́теля, я́ко вожа́, я́ко наста́вника, я́ко наказа́теля, я́ко проповѣ́дника, я́ко тобо́ю тмы избыхомъ, я́ко тобо́ю свѣт позна́хомъ. Тѣмъ чтемъ тя я́ко дѣ́лателя виногра́ду Христо́ву, я́ко те́рніе востерза́лъ еси́, идолослуже́ніе отъ земля́ Пе́рмьскіа, я́ко плугомъ, про́повѣдію взора́лъ еси́, я́ко сѣ́менемъ уче́ніемъ слове́съ кни́жныхъ насѣ́ялъ еси́ въ бразда́хъ серде́чныхъ, отню́ду же възраста́ютъ кла́сы добродѣ́тели, ихъ же, я́ко серпо́мъ вѣ́ры, сынове пе́рмстіи жнуть ра́достныя, и я́ко суши́ломъ воздержа́ніа сушаще, и я́ко цѣпы терпѣ́ніа млатя́ще, и я́ко въ жи́тницахъ душе́вныхъ соблюда́юще пшени́цу, тіи та́ко ядя́ть пи́щу неоску́дную...

So, O Bishop Stephen, the Permian land praises thee and honours thee as apostle, as teacher, as leader, as preceptor, as instructor, as preacher, since by thee they have been led out of darkness, since by thee they have seen the light. So we honour thee as a husbandman of Christ's vineyard who hast extirpated idolatry like weeds from the Permian land, hast ploughed the land with preaching as with a plough, with thy teaching of the word thou hast sown seed in the furrows of the heart, whence are growing the ears of virtue which the joyful sons of Perm' are reaping as with the sickle of faith, and drying as with the corn-drier of temperance, and threshing as with the flails of patience, and storing as in the granaries of the soul, and thus they receive nurture never-ending.

Two of the many features peculiar to this elaborate rhetoric are particularly striking: firstly, the author's predilection for compound words composed not only of two roots, e.g. доброутѣ́шенъ 'benignly consolatory', красносмотри́теленъ 'illustrious-looking', языко-вре́дный 'loose-tongued', but even of three, e.g. храбродобро-побѣ́дный 'valiantly-gloriously triumphant', каменнодельногра́д-ный 'having stone-built cities'; and secondly his predilection for pleonastic phrases, e.g. злозамы́шленное умышле́ніе 'evil-intentioned intention', скорообра́знымъ о́бразомъ 'in a swift-mannered manner', смиренному́дростью умудря́шеся 'he became wise [imperfect] with a humble wisdom', обновля́ху обновле́ніемъ 'they renewed [imperfect] with a renewing', паде́ніемъ падо́ша 'they fell [aorist] with a falling', etc. Ivan Timofeyev the official (дьякъ) and author of the well-known *Annals* (*Вре́менникъ*) of the Time of Troubles (1593–1613), defines this style as 'многокра́тно по то́нку реши—'to say repeatedly and subtly' [?]. Here, for instance, is his account of the division of Russia into the *zémshchina* and *opríchnina*[1] under Ivan IV the Terrible:

Отъ умышле́нія же зѣлныя я́рости на своя́ рабы́ подви́гся толи́къ, я́ко возненави́дѣ гра́ды земля́ своея́ вся и во гнѣвѣ свое́мъ раздѣле́ніемъ раздвое́нія еди́ны лю́ди раздѣли́ и я́ко двоевѣ́рны сотвори́, о́вы усвоя́я, о́вы же отмета́шася, я́ко чю́жи отрину́, не смѣ́ющимъ отню́дъ и́менемъ его́ мно́зѣмъ градо́мъ нарица́тися запреща́емомъ имъ, и всю зе́млю держа́вы своея́, я́ко сѣки́рою, на́полы нѣ́како разсѣче́.

He was so moved by an intention of great fury against his servants, that he conceived a hatred of the cities of his whole land, and in his anger divided by a separation into two groups people who were one, and treated them as if they were of two factions, taking some to himself while others were rejected [and] he cast them aside like strangers, many cities not daring by any means to call themselves by his name, being forbidden by him, and he thus cut all the land of his kingdom in two as if with a pole-axe.

These, however, are extreme examples. The normal narrative style of this time is simpler and less contorted, while still diverging considerably in its morphology and syntax from colloquial Russian, which filtered into literature only occasionally and in small doses. The typical literary language of the period is found, for instance, in the *Great Reading Minei* (*Вели́кие Че́тьи Мине́и*) compiled by the Metropolitan Makariy (born *c.* 1480), which was an established favourite of the Russian reader. Here is an excerpt from the life of St Iuar (19 October):

Утро же игемо́нъ повелѣ́ привести́ му́ченикы i, еди́ному оста́вшю въ темни́цѣ i отъ ранъ изнемо́гше, и рече́ имъ князь: се шесть, где седьмы́й? Тогда́ Иуаръ, разгорѣ́вся ду́хомъ святы́мъ, ставъ предъ кня́земъ, и рече́: тотъ бо у́мерлъ есть, азъ в него мѣ́сто хощю́ пострада́ти за Христа́. И рече́ князь: не прельща́йся Иуаре; а́ще ли, то мно́гыми му́ками живота́ гоньзне́ши. И рече́ Иуар: твори́, е́же хо́щеши. Разгнѣ́вавъ же ся царь, повелѣ́ на дре́вѣ повѣ́сити. И біахуть по всему́ тѣ́лу па́лицами. По семъ ногты желѣ́зны драхуть тѣ́ло его́ по ребро́мъ. И по семъ повелѣ́ стремгла́въ пригвозди́ти его́ на дре́вѣ, и

---

[1] Respectively, the areas left under the traditional control of the boyars, and th ose taken under the direct jurisdiction of the Tsar and controlled by means of his own punitive army, the *oprichniki*. [Ed.]

съдра́ти ко́жю съ хребта́ его́. И повелѣ́ сукова́тыми древы би́ти его́ и проби́ти утро́бу его́, до́ндежа испадо́ша вся вну́тренняа его́ на зе́млю.

And in the morning the governor ordered the martyrs to be brought to him, and one of them having stayed behind in the dungeon, having fainted from his wounds, (and) the prince said to them: 'There are six of you here, where is the seventh?' Then Iuar, inflamed by the Holy Ghost, stepped before the prince and said: 'He is dead. I want to suffer for Christ in his place.' And the prince said: 'Do not tempt Fate, Iuar, lest you lose your life in many torments.' And Iuar said: 'Do what you will.' The king becoming angry ordered that he should be hung on a tree. And they beat all his body with clubs. Then they tore his body about the ribs with iron hooks. And then he ordered him to be nailed head downward to a tree and to flay the skin from his back. And he ordered them to beat him with rough sticks and pierce his belly until all his intestines fell out on the ground.

The linguistic repertoire is more or less the same even where the laconic Biblical tone of narration gives way to something more emotive, as for instance in works with a military content. The account by Prince I. M. Katyryov-Rostovsky of the Time of Troubles (dated 1626) provides interesting examples, for instance of nature description:

Ю́же зимѣ́ проше́дши, вре́мя же бѣ приходитъ, я́ко со́лнце творя́ше подъ кру́гомъ зодѣ́йнымъ тече́ніе свое́, въ зоде́ю же вхо́дить Ове́нъ, въ ней же нощь со днемъ уровня́ется и весна́ пра́знуется, вре́мя начина́ется весели́ти сме́ртныхъ, на во́здусѣ свѣ́тлостію блиста́яся. Раста́явшу снѣ́гу и ти́ху вѣ́ющу вѣ́тру, и во простра́нные пото́кы исто́чницы протека́ютъ, тогда́ ра́тай ра́ломъ погружа́етъ и сла́дкую брозду́ прочерта́етъ и плодода́теля Бо́га на по́мощь призыва́етъ; расту́тъ желды, и зеленѣ́ютца поля́, и но́вымъ ли́ствіемъ облача́ютца древеса́, и отовсю́ду украша́ютца плоды́ земля́, пою́тъ пти́цы сла́дкимъ воспѣва́ніемъ, и́же по смотрѣ́нію Бо́жію и по Ево́ человѣколю́бію вся́кое упокое́ніе человѣ́комъ спѣ́етъ на услажде́ніе.

The winter already being past, the time had come when the sun was tracing its path through the circle of the zodiac, and Aries enters the zodiacal house in which night becomes equal with day and Spring is celebrated, the time begins for mortals to be gladdened, shining with radiance in the sky. The snow having melted and the soft wind blowing, (and) the rivers flow in broad streams, then the ploughman sinks his plough and traces a sweet furrow and calls on the munificent God for help; grasses grow and the fields turn green, and the trees become clothed in new foliage, and the fruits of the earth are luxuriant everywhere, the birds sing with a sweet song, and by God's providence and his love of mankind every comfort to men ripens for their delight.

Here, from the same source, is a stereotyped account of military operations:

Той же про́званный царе́вичь повелѣ́ во́йску своему́ препоя́сатися на брань и повелѣ́ врата́ гра́ду отвори́ти и та́ко спусти́ша брань ве́лію зѣло́. Царе́вы же воево́ды му́жески ополча́хуся проти́ву враго́въ царе́выхъ, и та́ко брань плитъ вéлія, падýтъ трýпіе мéртвыхъ сѣмо и овáмо. Царéвы же воевóды сѝлу восхищáютъ и устьì мечá гóнятъ, лю́діе же грáда тогó, хотя́тъ ли, не хотя́тъ ли, поля́ оставля́ютъ, и во градъ вхóдятъ и вратá грáду затворя́ютъ; и тáко отъ нихъ мнóзи на прáзѣ вратъ грáдныхъ умирáху, и вéліе падéніе бысть имъ.

This same so-called Tsarevich ordered his troops to harness themselves for battle and ordered the gates of the city to be opened, and so began a very great battle. But the Tsar's commanders fought valiantly against the Tsar's enemies, and so a great battle rages, and dead bodies are falling all around. And the Tsar's commanders seize the initiative and drive them with the points of their swords, and the people from the city fled willy-nilly from the field and entered the city and closed the gates of the city; and so many of them died on the threshold of the city gates and there was great loss of life among them.

As an example of publicist writing, here is an extract from the famous letter of Prince Andrey Kurbsky to Ivan IV ... :

Что провинѝли предъ тобóю, о цáрю! и чимъ прогнѣвали тя христіáнскіе предстáтели? Не прегóрдыя ли цáрства разорѝли и подрýчныхъ во всемъ тобѣ сотворѝли, мýжествомъ хрáбрости ихъ, у нихъ же прéжде въ рабóтѣ бьìша праотцьì нáши? Не претвéрдые ли грáды Гермáнскіе тщáніемъ рáзума ихъ от Бóга тобѣ даньì бысть? Сія ли намъ бѣднымъ воздáлъ есѝ, всерóдно погубля́я насъ? Или безсмéртенъ, цáрю! мнѝшись? Или въ небьìтную éресь прельщéнъ, áки не хотя́ ужé предстáти неумьìтному Судій богоначáльному Іисýсу, хотя́щему судѝти вселéннѣй въ прáвду, пáчеже прегóрдымъ мучѝтелемъ, и не обинýяся истязáти ихъ и до власъ прегрѣшéнія, я́ко же словесá глагóлютъ? ... Не испросѝхъ умилéнными глагóлы, ни умолѝхъ тя многослéзнымъ рыдáніемъ, и не исходáтайствовахъ от тебя́ никóеяжъ мѝлости архіерéйскими чинáми; и воздáлъ есѝ мнѣ зльìя за благíя и за возлюблéніе моé непримирѝтельную нéнависть! Кровь моя́, я́коже водá прóлитая за тя, вопíетъ на тя ко гóсподу моемý! ...

What wrong have they committed before you, O Tsar, and whereby have they, champions of Christianity, angered you? Have they not sacked the proudest kingdoms by the manliness of their courage and made them your subjects in all things, them to whom our forefathers were formerly in servitude? Have not the invincible German cities been given to you from God by their zeal and intelligence? Is it for these things you have recompensed us, unfortunates, by destroying all our kin? Do you think you are immortal, Tsar? Or are you seduced by vile heresy, as one no longer wishing to appear before the incorruptible Judge, all-powerful Jesus, who will judge the universe justly, and especially the arrogant tormentors, [and who] without compunction will interrogate them to the very hairs of their sins, as it is written? I have not besought you with plaintive words, nor supplicated with tearful sobbing, and I have not solicited from you any favour through the intercession of the archbishops, and you have repaid me with evil for good, and for my love with implacable hatred! My blood, spilt like water for you, cries out against you to my Lord!

These then are examples of the written language in its most common forms at the time when the Muscovite state was at its height. As before, it shows the blending of the learned and the colloquial strains, but if these excerpts are compared with those from earlier literary works, it becomes clear that the bookish element had become more firmly and consistently entrenched in the literary language, while the vernacular had at least gained no new ground. As a result, the former boundaries between the ecclesiastical–learned style and the literary had become less clear. While there is no doubt that in the realm of pronunciation and to some extent morphology the literary language of the 15th–17th centuries was considerably influenced by the living language, its vocabulary and syntax undoubtedly became more standardised, especially towards the end of the 16th and beginning of the 17th centuries. For example, in the 12th-century text of *Сказа́ние о Бори́се и Гле́бе* there are four times as many words of the type гра̀дъ, глава́, etc. as there are forms with полногла́сие—го́родъ, голова́, etc. In Katyryov-Rostovsky's narrative of 1626, however, there are ten to twelve times as many. In fact, in the whole of this fairly voluminous work the only pleophonic forms which occur are городо́къ (very rarely го́родъ, and almost consistently гра̀дъ), хоро́мы 'houses', переми́рие 'truce', напере́дъ 'henceforth' and шело́мы 'helmets'. In contrast to this it contains a vast number of words used exclusively in the Church Slavonic form, e.g. власы́ 'hair', врата́ 'gate', глава́ 'head', гла̀дъ 'hunger', мла̀дъ 'young', мра̀зъ 'frost', etc. A point of especial interest is the obvious striving to avoid the parallel use of both variants of a word.

We must add that the writers of the 15th–17th centuries had at their disposal an array of new lexical doublets which those of earlier periods did not have. One new type of opposition which had arisen was that of such words as жа́жа and жа́жда 'thirst', that is, with the correspondence between Russian ж and Bulgarian жд as reflexes of the prehistoric combination *dj* (cf. p. 8). At the period when the literary language was first making its appearance, the combination жд was impossible in Russian. Such words as the modern жда̀ть and три́жды were pronounced жьда̀ти and тришьды́ [i.e. each with three open syllables—cf. p. 42], and there was not a single word in which ж and д occurred in direct contiguity. As a result, Church Slavonic words containing the combination жд were not assimilated into Russian. This is why even in such writers as Kirill Turovsky we find поража́еть and not поражда́еть 'he strikes', and жа́жа and not жа́жда. In the Laurentian copy of *По́весть временны́х лет* there is not a single word with the Bulgarian consonant combination жд.

However, by the 15th century [through the loss of the *yers*] the pronunciation had changed from жьдати and тришьды to ждáти and трúжды. The combination жд had now become possible, and this paved the way for the infiltration of Bulgarian words of this type in the period of the second South Slavonic influence. They appear sporadically even in the 15th century, but become widespread only towards the end of the Muscovite period (Katyryov-Rostovsky already recognises мéжду 'between' and услаждéніе 'delectation', but still writes рассужéніе 'reasoning', грáжане 'citizens', вожь 'leader', etc.) Other examples of stylistic doublets of later date are вѣтеръ—вѣтръ 'wind', взлюбить—возлюбить 'fall in love with', etc.

Along with the literary style described above, the Muscovites were familiar with another style of written language, namely that of business. This style is traditionally called the chancellery language (прикáзный язы́к) since its most typical examples are to be found in official papers of the 16th–17th centuries—in government documents, legal deeds, business records, official and private correspondence, i.e. in all kinds of writing which have no pretensions to being literature. Here is the text of a grant charter of Grand Prince Vasiliy III dated 1505:

Се язъ князь велúки Васúлеи Ивáновичь всея Русíи пожáловалъ éсми Борúса Захáрьича Бороздинá да сы́на егó Ѳёдора, в Новотóржскомъ уѣздѣ, въ Жалинской губѣ, селóмъ Гавшинымъ съ деревнями, что бы́ло то селцó и деревни за Ондрéемъ за Слизневымъ въ помѣстьѣ, и съ обрóкомъ съ дéнежнымъ и съ хлѣбнымъ, и съ хлѣбомъ съ земны́мъ съ селѣтнимъ, и со всѣмъ съ тѣмъ, что къ тому селу́ и къ деревня́мъ из старины́ потя́гло: и кто у нихъ въ томъ селѣ и въ деревня́хъ живётъ людéй, и намѣстници мои́ Новотóржскіе и ихъ тіу́ни Борúса да сы́на егó Ѳёдора и тѣх ихъ людéй не су́дятъ ни въ чемъ, опрúчь душегу́бства и розбóа съ полú чнымъ, а правéтчики и довóдчики побóровъ у нихъ не беру́тъ, ни въѣзжа́ютъ ни всыла́ютъ къ нимъ нипочтó; а вѣдаетъ и су́дитъ Борúсъ да сынъ егó Ѳёдоръ свои́хъ людéй сáми во всемъ, и́ли кому́ прикáжутъ; а случи́тся судъ смѣснóй тѣмъ ихъ людемъ съ городски́ми людми́ и́ли съ волостны́ми, и намѣстници мои́ Новотóржскіе и их тіу́ни су́дятъ, а Борúсъ да сынъ егó Ѳёдоръ, и́ли ихъ прикáзщикъ, съ ни́ми жъ су́дитъ, а присудомъ дѣлятся по половúнамъ; а кому́ бу́детъ чегó искáти на Борúсѣ да на егó сы́нѣ Ѳёдорѣ, и́ли на ихъ прикáзщикѣ, инó ихъ сужу́ язъ князь велúки и́ли мой боя́ринъ введéной. А данá грáмота на Москвѣ лѣта 7014 Декабря́ 20 день.

Behold I, Grand Prince Vasiliy Ivanovich of all Russia have invested Boris Zakhar'ich Borozdin and his son Fyodor with the village of Gavshino with its hamlets, in Novotorzhok province, in Zhalinsk district, the which village and hamlets were the fief of Andrey Sliznev, along with the rents in money and kind, and with this year's crop on the ground, and with all that pertains to the said village and hamlets since long ago; and whoever of their people live in that village and hamlets, my governors in Novotorzhok and their officials have no jurisdiction whatever over Boris and his son Fyodor and their people, except for murder and robbery if caught red-handed, and my bailiffs and constables exact no taxes from them nor intrude upon nor send to them for any reason; and Boris and his son Fyodor govern and judge their people in everything themselves or through whomever they may appoint; and if a mixed court is held [to judge] their people along with people of the city or district, and my governors of Novotorzhok and their officials sit in judgment, and [if] Boris and his son Fyodor or their deputy sit in judgment along with them, the proceeds are to be divided equally; and if anyone shall have pretensions against Boris and his son Fyodor or against their deputy, then I the Grand Prince or my entrusted boyar will judge them. Document given in Moscow in the year 7014 on 20 December.

The following is an extract from a royal instruction of 1623:

И какъ къ тебѣ ся на́ша гра́мота при́детъ, и ты бъ на Устю́жнѣ на поса́дѣ и о́коло Устю́жны кото́рые лю́ди вино́ ку́рятъ и привозятъ къ Устю́жнѣ на прода́жу, а ины́е лю́ди и корчмы́ де́ржатъ, и́ли кото́рые лю́ди пи́ва ва́рятъ безъя́вочно, и ты бъ у тѣхъ люде́й то корче́мное, прода́жное и не я́вленое питьё и питухо́въ, и ви́нные суды, котлы́ и ку́бы велѣлъ вы́имати, не боя́сь никого́...А у кого́ корче́мное прода́жное питьё вы́мутъ вдругоря́дъ, и на тѣхъ лю́дехъ велѣлъ има́ти за́повѣди по пяти́ рублёвъ, а на питухѣхъ по полти́нѣ на человѣ́ка, а тѣхъ люде́й, у ково́ прода́жное питьё вы́мутъ въ другíе, велѣлъ мета́ти въ тюрьму́ дни на два и на три, а ис тюрьмы́ вы́нявъ, велѣлъ ихъ би́ти батоги́ неща́дно, чтобъ сто́ило кну́тья, а бивъ батоги́, велѣлъ ихъ подава́ти на крѣпкíе пору́ки з за́письми въ томъ, что имъ впередъ прода́жного питья́ не держа́ти и никаки́мъ воровство́мъ не ворова́ти.

And when this our document reaches you, then those people who distil liquor in the township of Ustyuzhna and around Ustyuzhna and bring it to sell in Ustyuzhna and others who keep illicit taverns or brew beer without a licence, then you are to order their illicit beverages, saleable and undeclared, and their tipplers, and their liquor vessels, boilers and stills, to be seized without let or hindrance...And anyone who has his illicit saleable liquor taken from him for the second time, then order such persons to be fined five roubles each, and their tipplers half a rouble each, and those whose saleable liquor shall be taken on further occasions, order to be thrown into prison for two or three days, and when they are taken out of prison order them to be beaten mercilessly with sticks, so that it is as good as a flogging (?), and having beaten them with sticks, order them to undertake firm guarantees with signatures to the effect that they must not stock saleable liquor in future and must not rob [the excise?] in any way.

Letters written by peasants in the 17th century show another aspect of business correspondence. The following petition was submitted to the boyar F. I. Sheremetev in 1639:

Госуда́рю Ѳёдору Iва́новичю бьётъ чело́мъ сто́льника Алексѣ́я Ники́тича Годуно́ва, во́тчины ево́, села́ Нико́льскаго харче́вничишко Сергу́нька Артемьевъ сынъ Торховъ, жа́лоба, госуда́рь, мнѣ на твоево́, госуда́рева на бобыля́, во́тчины твое́й, госуда́ревы села́ Покро́вскаго на Каза́рина Михаилова сы́на: в ны́нѣшнемъ, госуда́рь, в 147-мъ году́, декабря́ въ 18-й де. в ночи́ и покра́лъ, госуда́рь, тотъ Каза́ринъ оу меня́ сироту́ а спрова́лся бы́ло оу меня́ ночева́ть, а оукра́лъ, госуда́рь, мани́сто, а мани́сту цена́ полтора́ рубли́, да серги́, цена́ серга́мъ со́рокъ алты́нъ, да каѳта́нъ свитно́й, цена́ два́тцать алты́нъ, да рукави́цы бора́новые с варе́ги, да на два алты́на колаче́й, да три рубли́ де́негъ... Оуми́лостивися госуда́рь Ѳёдор Ива́новичъ, пожа́луй, вели́, госуда́рь, на того́ своево́ бобыля́ дать свои́ пра́ведноі судъ и оупра́ву в тоі ги́бели. Госуда́рь, сми́луйся, пожа́луй.

To my lord Fyodor Ivanovich a humble petition from Sergun'ka son of Artyom of Torkhov (?), innkeeper in the village of Nikol'skoye of the estate of the nobleman Aleksey Nikitich Godunov, I have a complaint, master, against Kazarin son of Mikhail, your lordship's peasant of your lordship's village of Pokrovskoye of your estate: [that] in the present year 147 [i.e. 7147 since the Creation] on the 18th day of December at night the said Kazarin did steal from me, lord, poor orphan that I am, he had arranged to spend the night at my place, and stole, my lord, a necklace, the value of the necklace being one and a half roubles, and earrings, the value of the earrings being 120 kopecks, and a coat-kaftan value sixty kopecks, and sheepskin mittens with woollen linings, and loaves worth six kopecks, and three roubles in cash... Be gracious, my lord Fyodor Ivanovich, have pity, and order, my lord, your peasant to receive his just deserts and retribution for this loss. My lord, have mercy I pray.

The following petition (челоби́тная) belongs to the 1670s, and was submitted to Sheremetev's successor as owner of the village of Pokrovskoye (in Galich district of what was later to become Kostroma province)—Prince N. I. Odoyevsky and his son:

Госуда́рю, кня́зю Ники́тѣ Ива́новичю и госуда́рю, кня́зю Якову Ники́тичю бие́тъ чело́мъ сирота́ вашъ, госуда́ревъ Га́лицкие во́тчины, села́ Покро́вского, дере́вни Ка́рпова Улья́нко Кири́ловъ: судо́мъ Бо́жиимъ, по грѣхо́мъ свои́мъ, овдовѣ́лъ по друго́му го́ду и сталъ без пристро́ю, а жена́тъ былъ двема́, а тре́тьево не моли́твятъ, а тро́е ребяти́шекъ, и живу́чи живо́ть свой му́чю, робяти́шки малы́, другъ дру́гу не посо́битъ, а земли́ подо мно́ю десети́на съ че́тью, а живота́ одна́ клече́нко, а бо́льше того́ живота́ нѣтъ ничево́, і пить, ѣсти нѣчево, хлѣбъ не роди́лся...

To my lord Prince Nikita Ivanovich and my lord Prince Yakov Nikitich a humble petition from your poor orphan Ul'yanko Kirilov of the hamlet of Karpov of the village of Pokrovskoye of your lordship's estate of Galich: by God's judgment and for my sins I became a widower two years ago and became destitute. I have been married twice, and they will not marry any one a third time, and [I have] three children, and I work my livestock to death, the children are little, one cannot help the other, and I have one and a quarter desyatins of land, and of livestock one miserable horse, and apart from this I have no other livestock and nothing to drink or eat, the harvest is poor, etc.

Clearly the language of these documents and petitions differs greatly from that of contemporary literary works. It is entirely colloquial, without Church Slavonicisms or archaic forms. In the second excerpt, for instance, we find на питухѣхъ, whereas in the learned language, if the word were ever used there, we would expect to find на питусѣхъ. In both documents the modern past tense forms only are used. The syntax is crude and rambling, without well-rounded sentences and without such constructions as the dative absolute.

The sharp contrast between these two types of written language, and the clear demarcation line between their functions, are the most characteristic features of this period. The important thing is that this demarcation line was truly functional—that is, the choice for composing a given text was determined mainly by the genre and character of the text, and not by such factors as the educational standard of the writer or his social position or profession. At best, such factors could only have secondary significance. As a general rule a [literate] person could switch freely from the refined literary language to the business style whenever circumstances demanded. We have already seen the language used by Prince Kurbsky in his letter to Ivan IV, but here is how he wrote in a letter addressed to the Monastery of the Caves:

Вы́мите бо́га ра́ди поло́жено писа́ніе подъ пе́чью, стра́ха ра́ди сме́ртнаго. А пи́сано въ Пече́ры, одно́ въ столбце́хъ, а друго́е в тетра́тяхъ; а поло́жено подъ пе́чью в ызбу́шке въ мое́и въ ма́лои; пи́сано дѣ́ло госуда́рское. И вы то отошли́те лю́бо къ госуда́рю, а лю́бо ко Пречи́стои въ Пече́ры. Да оста́лися тетра́тки переплетены́, а ко́жа на нихъ не поло́жена, и вы и тѣхъ бо́га ра́ди не затеря́ите.

For God's sake take out the papers hidden under the stove, for fear of death. They are addressed to the [Monastery of] the Caves, one in scrolls and the other in book form; and they are hidden under the stove in my little house; it is a matter of state that is written there. So send it either to the Tsar or to the [Church of?] the Immaculate Virgin in the Caves. Also there are some bound books, without leather on them, for God's sake don't lose these either.

The chancellery language was used not only for documents and letters, but sometimes for works of much larger size, if the subject-matter was appropriate. One such work, published moreover in printed form, was the *Law Code* (*Уложе́ніе*) of 1649. The slight traces of learned influence which it bears are to be explained by the special circumstances surrounding its appearance, particularly the fact that it was to be printed. The verbose practical chapters of *Домостро́й* (*The House Orderer*), however, are completely devoid of any learned flavour. The contents list shows, for instance:

Оука́зъ клю́чнику ка́къ держа́ти на по́гребе запа́съ просо́лнои и в бо́чкахъ, и в кла́дахъ и в мѣ́рникахъ и во тча́нахъ и в веде́рцахъ, мя́со, ры́ба, капу́ста, огурцы́, сьли́вы, лимо́ны, икра́, ры́жики, гру́зди; О томъ же ко́ли што коу́питъ

Literary language in the 15th–17th centuries

оу когó селъ нѣтъ и вся́кои домáшнеи обихóдъ и лѣ́те и зимѣ́ и какъ запасáти в годъ и дóма живóтина вся́кая води́ть, и ѣ́ства и питиé держáти всегды́.

Instructions to the butler on how to keep in the cellar stores of salted produce in barrels and in boxes and in measures and in tubs and in buckets—meat, fish, cabbage, cucumbers, plums, lemons, caviare, saffron milk-cap and pepper-cap mushrooms; [and] about the best time for buying various things for anyone who has no estates, and all manner of domestic routine both in summer and winter, and how to store up for the year and keep all manner of livestock at home and always to have food and drink.

Unlike the earlier period in the history of written Russian, the system of styles illustrated here lacks an intermediate category, that is, a style representing the blending of the two extreme styles described. In fact the conditions for such a compromise did not occur for some time in the Muscovite state. However, by the second half of the 17th century the possibility of a third style was becoming a reality. The important changes connected with this make a clear division between the old and the modern periods in the history of the language, since they lead to the birth of the Russian national standard language.

8

TOWARDS A SINGLE RUSSIAN
LANGUAGE

During the whole Old Russian period a struggle had been taking place in the language between the two conflicting tendencies of regionalism and centralism. The evidence suggests that the differences between the various dialects of Old Russian were not so great as to hinder mutual intelligibility. Moreover, a powerful influence towards unity was present in the heritage of Church Slavonic as one of the basic sources of the written language, since by its nature it occupied a position above or at least common to all the dialects. Despite all these factors, however, it is essential to bear in mind that the Old Russian written language, whether in its ecclesiastical–learned, its business or its literary style, was a language based on dialects, so that we can speak of the written languages of Kiev, of Novgorod, of Ryazan', of Pskov or of Moscow. But it is obvious that the development of a centralised Russian state was bound to lead to the defeat of centrifugal tendencies in the language also. The rise and establishment of the autocratic Muscovite state on the ruins of feudal disunity was bound to prepare the way for the appearance of a single, centralised, national language.

The national language grew from the same territorial and cultural roots as the Russian state itself—it was founded on the spoken language of the city of Moscow and the written language of the Muscovite chancelleries. As the provincial chancelleries gradually adopted the orthography and terminology used in Moscow, and the Moscow civil servants accepted certain provincial elements into their everyday language, the language of the Moscow chancelleries (прика́зы) attained the status of the universal language of the state. (So far as the *spoken* language is concerned, of course, the tendency towards centralisation was at this time still very weak.)

In the second half of the 17th century, however, the general trends of cultural and political development in Russia were creating a need for a language which would be universal not only in the territorial sense, but also in its function as the general written language. In order to fulfil this need, the official language of the state had to acquire qualities which only a literary language could provide. It was on these grounds that there arose the complex and prolonged process of competition and mutual adaptation between the basic varieties of the Old Russian written language, which in the end produced the modern literary language.

This process was induced, among other things, by significant developments in Russian literature [in the widest sense] as the reflection of the political, economic and cultural changes taking place in Russian life in general at the end of the 17th and beginning of the 18th centuries. This period saw the emergence of various types of book for which the existing system of two styles of language was proving inadequate. These were principally on such subjects as economics, technology, and science—technical literature in the widest sense, which in certain respects really was *literature*, that is it demanded a certain level of expository style suitable for printing and reading. The great number of translated works was a factor of enormous importance. The translators had to adapt the old language of business not only to the demands of literate exposition but at the same time to the linguistic conventions of western European civilisation. As a result the business language of the end of the 17th century, and even more so that of the beginning of the 18th, is very different from that of the old chancellery documents. It is far more literary, containing elements absorbed from the old learned style and many international terms derived from Greek and Latin which it had taken over from western Europe, sometimes with considerable ostentation.

One of the earliest examples of this quasi-literary business style is Kotoshikhin's *Записки* (1667), a work which gives a vivid picture of official and personal life in Russia in the reign of Aleksey Mikhaylovich. For the most part it is written in the old-fashioned business style, e.g.

ѐствы ж обы́чай гото́вить по́просту, безъ пріпра́въ, безъ я́годъ и са́хару и бесъ пе́рцу и инби́рю и ины́хъ спо́собовъ, малосо́лны и безу́ксусны. А какъ начну́тъ ѐсті, і въ то вре́мя ѐствы ста́вятъ на столъ по одному́ блю́ду, а ины́е ѐствы прино́сятъ съ пова́рни и де́ржатъ въ рука́хъ лю́ді ихъ, і въ кото́рой ѐствѣ ма́ло у́ксусу и со́ли и пе́рцу, і въ тѣ ѐствы приба́вливаютъ на столѣ, а быва́етъ вся́кихъ ѐствъ по 50 и по 100.

6-2

They usually prepare food simply, without seasoning, without berries or sugar, and without pepper, ginger or other things, little-salted and without vinegar. And when they begin a meal, they place one dish on the table at a time, and their servants bring other dishes from the kitchen and hold them in their hands, and to dishes that contain little vinegar or salt or pepper they add [them when they are already] on the table, and they have fifty or a hundred dishes of various kinds.

Or, in another place:

И по́сле того́ зго́вору жени́хъ прове́даетъ про то́е неве́сту, и́ли кто съ стороны́, хотя́ то́е неве́сту взять за себя́ и́лі за сы́на, наро́чно тому́ жениху́ розобьётъ, что она́ в де́встве своёмъ нечиста́, и́ли глуха́, или нема́, и́ли уве́чна, и что нибудь худо́е за не́ю прове́даетъ, и́ли ска́жутъ, и тотъ челове́къ то́е неве́сты за себя́ не возьмётъ, то́е неве́сты оте́цъ и́ли мать бьютъ чело́мъ о томъ патриа́рху, что онъ по за́говору своему́ и по заря́ду то́е неве́сты на срокъ не взялъ, і взя́ті не хо́четъ, и те́мъ ее́ обесче́стилъ... А е́желі за того́ челове́ка неве́ста приде́тъ де́вства своего́ не сохрани́ла, и тотъ жени́хъ, ве́дая свою́ жену, къ царю́ чело́мъ уда́рить не е́здитъ, потому́ что ужъ царю́ до его́ прие́зду объя́вятъ, и онъ его́ к себе́ на о́чи пусти́ть не вели́тъ.

And after this contract [is made] the bridegroom finds out about his fiancée, or someone else wishing to take this girl for himself or for his son, will tell the bridegroom on purpose, that she is not a virgin, or that she is deaf or dumb or crippled, and they find out or say something bad about her, and [then] the man will not accept his bride, [then] the father or mother of the girl make a petition to the Patriarch that he [the bridegroom] has not taken and will not take the bride at the appointed time according to his contract and agreement, and has thereby dishonoured her... And if a bride comes to the man without her maidenhead, then the husband, having had intercourse with his wife, does not go to petition the Tsar, because the Tsar will have been informed before he arrives, and will refuse to grant him an audience.

But in certain passages of Kotoshikhin's *Запи́ски* other [more sophisticated] stylistic tendencies appear, e.g.

А лу́читца царю́ мысль свою́ о чемъ объяви́ти, и онъ имъ объявя́, прика́зываетъ, чтобъ они́, боя́ре и ду́мные лю́ді, помы́сля, къ тому де́лу да́ли спо́собъ: и кто исъ тѣхъ боя́ръ побо́лши и разу́мнѣе, и́ли кто і изъ ме́ншихъ, и они́ мысль свою́ къ спо́собу объя́вливаютъ; а ины́е боя́ре бра́ды свои́ уста́вя, ничего́ не отвѣща́ютъ, потому́ что царь жа́луетъ мно́гихъ въ боя́ре не по ра́зуму ихъ, но по вели́кой поро́де, и мно́гие изъ нихъ гра́моте не учёные и не студеро́ванные, одна́ко сы́щется и окро́мѣ ихъ кому бы́ті на отвѣ́ты разу́мному изъ бо́лшихъ и изъ ме́ншихъ стате́й боя́ръ.

If the Tsar desires to make a pronouncement on some matter, then announcing it to them he commands that they, the boyars and counsellors, having considered it, should decide on a way for dealing with this matter; and the boyars, those of greater status and intelligence, and those of lower, announce their view of ways and means; but some boyars, sticking out their beards, make no reply, because the Tsar invests many as boyars not because of their intelligence, but because of high breeding, and many of them are illiterate and unschooled; however even without them there are found some among the greater and lesser ranks of the boyars capable of giving an intelligent answer.

How the new business language evolved later can be seen even by comparing the preceding examples with extracts from Peter I's newspaper *Ведомости*, such as the following report from the fourth issue in 1704:

На Москвѣ салдáтская женá родилá жéнска пóлу младéнца мёртва о дву главáхъ, и тѣ глáвы отъ другъ дрýга отдѣленьí осóбь, и со всѣми своими состáвы и чýвствы совершéнны, а рýки и нóги и всё тѣло такъ, какъ единому человѣку прирóдно имѣти. И по анатóмии усмóтрены в немъ два сéрдца соединёны, двѣ пéчени, два желýдка и два гóрла. О чёмъ и отъ учёныхъ мнóгie удивляются.

In Moscow a soldier's wife gave birth to a still-born baby of female sex with two heads, and these two heads are quite separate, and perfect in all its parts and faculties, and its arms and legs and whole body are as it is normal for one person to have. And on dissection it was found to have two hearts joined together, two livers, two stomachs and two throats. Which astonishes even many scholars.

No. 14 for 1719 contains the following report from Rome:

Въ прóшлой втóрникъ пpinцéссa Собиéская вступя въ своé 17 лѣто, комплиментóвана былá о томъ отъ мнóгixъ знáтныхъ осóбъ обóixъ полóвъ; О томъ же отпрáвiли торжéственную обéдню въ цéрквѣ Урселiнскои съ концéртомъ сѣлó увеселiтельнои симѳóнiи на гласáхъ i инструмéнтахъ; Пáпа послáлъ къ неи презéнтъ состоящеи въ 1000 золотьíxъ тáлерахъ. Кардинáлъ Аквавiва тáкже трактовáлъ богáто за обéдомъ мнóгixъ Аглiнскихъ Госпóдъ и дамъ, а пóслѣ обéда óная пpinцéссa ѣздiла веселiтiся на зáгороднои дворъ зовóмои Лодовiзiя, гдѣ онá принятá отъ Дуцéссы Фiано и княжньí Полестрiны дщéри княгiни Пiомбiны.

Last Tuesday Princess Sobieska having her seventeenth birthday was congratulated on it by notable people of both sexes. A solemn mass was celebrated in the Ursuline church with a concert [consisting] of a very entertaining symphony for voices and instruments. The Pope sent her a present consisting of 1,000 gold dollars. Cardinal Aquaviva also treated many English gentlemen and ladies to a rich dinner, and after the dinner the Princess went to enjoy herself at the country house called Lodovisi where she was received by the Duchess Fiano and Princess Palestrina the daughter of Princess Piombini.

As a good example of the new learned style which was emerging in technical literature parallel to the official style illustrated above, we may take the following preface to the translation of Varenius's *Geographia* published by Fyodor Polikarpov in 1718. The translator writes:

Моя дóлжность объявiти, яко преводихъ сiю [книгу] не на сáмый высóкiй славéнский дiалéктъ прóтивъ áвторова сочинéнiя и хранéнiя прáвилъ граммати́ческихъ, но мнóжае граждáнскаго посрéдственнаго употребля́лъ нарѣ́чiя, охраня́я сенсъ и рѣчи оригинáла иноязьíчнаго. Речéнiя же терминáльная грéческая и латiнская оставля́хъ не преведенá рáди лýчшаго въ дѣлѣ знáнiя, а инá преведенá объявля́хъ, заключáя въ паранѳéси.

Towards a single Russian language

It is my duty to announce that I have translated this book not into the most elevated Slavonic dialect in accordance with the author's composition and observance of the rules of [Latin] grammar, but have used many things from the average secular form of speech, preserving the sense and import (?) of the foreign original. Greek and Latin technical terms I have left untranslated for the sake of a better understanding of the subject, and those which I have translated I have indicated by enclosing them in parenthesis.

Not only the language of this preface, but the author's view of the language he is using, is highly significant. He considers it to be not (Church) Slavonic (славе́нский), but 'average secular' or 'civil' style. From the time of Peter I onwards 'славе́нский язы́к' gradually comes to mean the ecclesiastical language. This is the result of the emancipation of Russian secular culture from the Church, so that for the first time in history Russian society began to understand that the business and learned styles of previous centuries were literally two different languages. Much later, when this view had become widely adopted, the term 'Church Slavonic' (церковнославя́нский) was coined to describe the traditional language of the ecclesiastical writings and related works of Old Russian literature. This same realisation gave rise to Peter I's reform of the Russian alphabet [in 1708–10] which separated the ecclesiastical script from the civil alphabet.

With regard to the 'гражда́нское посре́дственное наре́чие' which Polikarpov contrasts with 'высо́кий славе́нский язы́к', it is quite clear even from the passage quoted that it is in fact much closer to the language of the Church than to that of the old chancelleries. This then is a new business language, based upon the blending of the two old varieties of written language. How and in what proportions this blending should take place, however, became clear only as time went on. The essential difference between this new language of business, with its 'bookish' element in evidence to a greater or lesser degree depending upon circumstances, and the old official language, was that the new one aspired to a standard of *literacy*, whereas previously this concept was associated only with the ecclesiastical language and the literary works based upon it. It is not surprising, therefore, that in the time of Peter I the term 'славе́нский язы́к на́шего шти́ля'—'the Slavonic language of our usage'—was sometimes used to describe the secular language which, while it observed the same norms of literacy as the ecclesiastical language, was distinct from it.

The question of literacy, i.e. of a way of writing governed by certain rules, is of great importance for an understanding of the process which led to the appearance of a national standard language. Russian literacy had grown up on the basis of the ecclesiastical language, and it was this standard of literacy which provided the basis for linguistic development in the post-Petrine age. A very important part in this process was played by the linguistic standards of south-west Russia where, at a much earlier period than in Muscovy, scholars and writers had begun to concern themselves with the study of Church Slavonic and with its refinement as a medium of literary expression. Russian literature and scholarship of the end of the 17th and beginning of the 18th centuries owe a considerable debt to a whole galaxy of diligent scholars of Ukrainian and Belorussian origin.[1] A grammar by Meletiy Smotritskiy (*Граматіки Славенскиᴙ правилное сѵнтагма*), originally published in Lithuania in 1619, was printed in a revised edition in Moscow in 1648. Naturally it was based on Church Slavonic. Republished in 1721, this became the standard grammar book in Russia right up till the end of the 18th century. Peter I's overt enmity towards the church did not blind him to the enormous importance of a knowledge of Church Slavonic grammar as a guide to correct usage in Russian.

Naturally, at this period there could be no question of complete literacy in the modern sense. Private and personal documents lag far behind official documents and especially printed books in the general movement towards a regularised middle style of literate writing. Peter I's own language is considerably less literate than that of his chancelleries, with spelling based on much earlier traditions. Here, for instance, is an excerpt from a decree of 25 April 1707 written in the Tsar's own hand:

В добаѳъку. Крóмѣ пѣшихъ ещё двѣ тысячи человѣкъ собрáть кóнныхъ, а скóлкихъ дворóѳъ íли inákимъ óбразомъ, о томъ разверстáть с савѣту, а сóбраныхъ зачéсть в укáзное числó, тóлко худыхъ i зелó стáрыхъ выкинуть, тáкже чтобъ отнюдь iз кресьянъ нé было, но ѳсѣ iз дваровыхъ, под кáзнью... С посáтскихъ тысяча двѣсте человѣкъ, i брать на нихъ жáлованья по тринáтцати рублёѳъ человѣку на годъ.[2]

[1] The reconquest (from Poland) in the middle of the 17th century of a part of the Ukraine brought to Moscow the beneficial influence of Ukrainian scholars educated in the more sophisticated cultural atmosphere of the Polish- and western-orientated Kiev Academy, such as Simeon Polotsky and Stefan Yavorsky. [Ed.]

[2] Note the reflection of such phonetic features as devoiced consonants: ф instead of в in добавку, дворов, все, рублев; т for д in посадских; and аканье: а instead of о in совету, дворовых. [Ed.]

Moreover. Apart from the infantry, two thousand more cavalrymen are to be assembled, (and) how many homesteads or in what other way must be allocated by a council, and those assembled to be counted among the number indicated, only the useless and very old to be rejected, also there must not be any at all from the peasantry, but all from among the household serfs, under pain of execution... One thousand two hundred men from the towns, and you are to take for them pay at the rate of thirteen roubles per man per year.

The norms [of spelling] which nevertheless existed are eloquently described by an observant foreign traveller Wilhelm Ludolf, whose grammar of Russian (*Grammatica Russica*) was published in Oxford in 1696. Here we read [the original is in Latin]: 'the majority of Russians, in order not to seem illiterate, write words not as they pronounce them, but as they should be pronounced according to the rules of Slavonic grammar, so that they write e.g. сегодня *segodnia* "today" although they pronounce it севодни *sevodni*'. Obviously this remains true till the present day, despite the determined and capable attempt made to rebel against it as early as 1748 by V. K. Trediakovsky in his *Разговóр об ортогрáфии старúнной и нóвой*. This treatise, suggested to Trediakovsky by French 16th–17th-century models, exhorts its readers to make a complete break with the traditions of Church Slavonic grammar and adopt a manner of writing which would reflect contemporary speech. Trediakovsky declares that one should write not 'according to the root' or 'derivation', but 'according to articulation' (по óргану), 'according to the sounds' (по звóнам). He foretells the future triumph of his ideas in the following quaint phrases, which we reproduce in the spelling invented by Trediakovsky himself:

Я не отчаяваюсь, чтобъ въ нѣкоторое время не сталi всѣ у насъ пiсать, ешче i учоныi, iзъ которыхъ катоноватѣйшіi, позвольте учоное слово, наiбольше хорохорятся протiвъ своновъ. Нѣжный дамскiй выговоръ давно уже у насъ своны наблюдаетъ. А дамы кого себѣ не заставятъ, не прiсiлiвая впрочемъ, послѣдовать? Iбо i господа учоныi веть не деревяныi.

I do not despair that after some time everyone in our country will write [thus], even the scholars, the most Cato-like of whom, excuse the learned word, are most vehement against the sounds. The tender pronunciation of the ladies has for long observed the sounds. And whom can the ladies not cause to follow them, without indeed forcing? For even the learned gentlemen are not made of wood.

And indeed 'ladies' spelling' (дáмская орфогрáфия) did remain in everyday use for a long time, so that, for instance, in the well-known *Запúски* of Natal'ya Dolgorukaya (1767) we find the spellings канешно (конéчно), пожмеіотъ (пожмёт), сщастия (счáстья), где глупь, где мель и где мошна пристать (где глубь, где мель и где мóжно пристáть), ничего нихто не знаитъ (ничегó никтó не знáет), etc. But Trediakovsky's scheme proved to be too utterly Utopian, and even he himself did not follow it boldly and consistently, since, apart from anything else, his spelling undoubtedly reflects a bookish type of pronunciation and not that of living speech. Trediakovsky's triumphant rival, the redoubtable Lomonosov, took up a definite stand on the side of tradition in language, and, notwithstanding numerous instances of change and hesitation since then, this was the approach which history proved to be the only viable one.

Let us now consider the part played by literature proper in this movement towards a standard language of middle style. At first it had only a subordinate role. The end of the 17th and beginning of the 18th centuries was a profoundly critical period in Russian literature and in the attitudes of writers. We cannot do justice to all sides of this important problem here, but we must note the effects of this crisis in the sphere of the written language. A writer of the preceding period might be literate to a greater or lesser degree, might observe more or less strictly the established linguistic norms or make concessions to his own everyday colloquial usage, but he was always at least aware that such norms existed. They were inculcated on the basis of the prayer-book (*Часослóв*) and the Psalter, and could be observed in such literary works as the *Четьи минéи*. Some idea of the innate attitude of a bookman of the pre-Petrine era towards these norms can be gleaned from the preface to the 1648 edition of Smotritsky's *Grammar* or the preface to the *Psalter* published in Moscow in 1645. Among the exhortations in the latter, addressed specifically to teachers and pupils, we read:

Подобáетъ ýбо вамъ о учи́теліе вѣдѣти, кáко вамъ младьíхъ дѣтéй учи́ти божéственнымъ письменéмъ, пéрвое бо въ начáлѣ бýквамъ, си́рѣчь áзбуцѣ, потóмъ же, часóвники и псалтыри́, и прóчія божéственныя кни́ги; и пáче же ýбо всегó, éже бы вамъ наказáти и изучи́ти ученикóмъ áзбука чи́сто и пря́мо по существý, кáко котóрое слóво рѣчію зовéтся, и неспѣшно. А и сами́мъ бы вамъ знáти же естествó словéсъ, и си́лу ихъ разумѣти и гдѣ говори́ти дебéло и тóностно, и гдѣ с пригибéніемъ устъ и гдѣ с раздвижéніемъ, и гдѣ прóсто.

Therefore it is proper for you, o teacher, to know how you should teach young children the Holy Scriptures, in the first place the letters, that is to say the alphabet, and then the Book of Hours and Psalter and other divine books; and so above all if you are to instruct and teach your pupils the alphabet properly and directly according to its nature [you should know] what each letter is called in speech, without haste. And you yourself must know the essence of words, and understand their power and where one should pronounce voiced (?) and unvoiced (?), and where with closing of the lips and where with opening, and where simply.

The preface goes on to point out that ѣ must not be confused with e, gives rules for stress, and so on. The language of the books which formed the basis of this scholastic approach was canonised for future generations, especially after the activity of the Patriarch Nikon[1] and the publication of the corrected version of the Bible in 1663, and may be considered in its way the definitive form of Church Slavonic. It was this language that Lomonosov had in mind when he wrote his influential work *О пóльзѣ книгъ церькóвныхъ въ Россíйскомъ языкѣ* in 1748.

But the literature of the end of the 17th and beginning of the 18th centuries is more notable for its deviation from these models than for its adherence to them. Even in works which are essays in spiritual eloquence and apologetics two extreme tendencies appear: either their authors indulge in forms of 'извíтие словéс' so extreme that even contemporary rhetoricians like Polikarpov were moved to complain of their 'extravagant Slavonicism' (необыкновéнная славéнщизна) and Hellenism (еллинѝзм), or else they favour innovation—the use of Latin and western European words and phrases, a preference for vernacular rather than bookish forms, etc. Thus we find Stefan Yavorsky, in his address to the Psalmist David,[2] using the phrase: Поклонѝ тóлько ýши въ глагóлы устъ человѣ́ческихъ: колѝку слáву ѝмаши за твоé мужествó, крѣ́пость и трудьí кавалéрскіе 'Only bend thine ears to the words of human lips; how much glory thou hast because of thy manliness, courage and chivalrous deeds' [the word кавалерскіе is out of style]. In another sermon we read: Вѝдиши ли сію́ женý; а что жъ ту, Спасѝтелю мой, въ той жéнщинѣ зрѣ́нія достóйно; не вѝжу я въ ней ничтó же удивѝтельно; áще томý велѝшъ присмáтриватися, что хорошó устрóилася, червленѝцею и бѣлѝломъ лицó умастѝла, *челó своé, что кóжу на барабáнѣ, вьíтянула*...'Dost thou see this woman? What is there here, my Saviour, worthy of sight in this woman? I see nothing astounding in her, unless thou commandest

---

[1] Patriarch 1652–66, whose reforms in texts and liturgy were a major factor in bringing about the Schism in the Russian church. [Ed.]

[2] Stefán Yávorsky (1655–1722), Metropolitan of Ukrainian origin who wrote sermons and poems in Slavonic and Latin. [Ed.]

me to take notice that she is well-formed, has smeared her face with rouge and powder [and] has drawn her forehead as tight as the skin of a drum...' [the last phrase is obviously inappropriate]. In sermons by Feofan Prokopovich[1] such phrases as the following frequently appear: А ты, но́вый и новоца́рствующий гра́де Петро́въ, не высо́кая ли сла́ва еси́ фунда́тора твоего́ 'And thou, new and new-reigning city of Peter, art thou not the great glory of thy founder?', or: Не довлѣ́ютъ вои́стину пресла́вной о́ной викто́ріи ти́сяща устъ ри́торскихъ, и не преста́нутъ сла́вити вѣ́ки мно́гія, донелѣ́же міръ стои́тъ 'Truly a thousand poets' mouths are insufficient for this most glorious victory, and its praises shall not cease to be sung for many ages as long as the earth stands', or: Перегрина́ція еди́на все то́е какъ на дла́нѣ показу́етъ, и живу́ю геогра́фію въ па́мяти напису́етъ, такъ что человѣ́къ не ина́че свѣ́данные стра́ны въ мы́сли свое́й имѣ́етъ, а́ки бы на во́здусѣ лета́я имѣ́лъ о́ные предъ о́чима. 'One journey shows all this as if on the palm of one's hand, and depicts the living geography in the memory so that a man bears the countries studied in his thoughts exactly as if, flying in the air, he had them before his eyes'. [In these quotations the inappropriate words are the Latinisms фунда́торъ, викто́рія and перегрина́ція.] There is an interesting transition to everyday language in Prokopovich's *Похва́льное сло́во о фло́те* (*Panegyric Oration on the Fleet*) of 1720:

А въ пе́рвыхъ, поне́же не къ еди́ному мо́рю прилежи́тъ предѣ́лами свои́ми сія́ мона́рхія, то какъ не бесчестно ей не имѣ́ть фло́та. Не сы́щемъ ни еди́ной въ свѣ́тѣ дере́вни, кото́рая, надъ рѣ́кою и́ли е́зеромъ поло́жена, не имѣ́ла бы ло́докъ...Стои́мъ надъ водо́ю и смо́тримъ, какъ го́сти къ намъ прихо́дятъ, а са́ми того́ не умѣ́емъ. Сло́во въ сло́во такъ, какъ въ стіхотво́рскихъ фа́булахъ нѣ́кій Танта́лъ стои́тъ въ водѣ́, да жа́ждетъ. И потому́ и на́ше мо́ре не на́ше...

And firstly, in so far as this kingdom is bounded by several seas, how then should it not be a dishonour for it not to have a fleet? We shall not find a single village on earth which if it is situated on a river or lake, does not have boats... We stand at the water's edge and watch merchants coming and going, while we ourselves are unable to do this. It is just as in the poetic fables a certain Tantalus stands in the water but thirsts. And thus even our own sea is not ours...

Nevertheless, high-flown rhetoric rooted in medieval 'извитие словес', but reinforced by fashionable learned expressions from western Europe, still predominates. Here is one of the later echoes of

---

[1] Feofán Prokopóvich (1681–1736), Ukrainian Archbishop of Novgorod who collaborated with Peter I in his reforms and wrote sermons, poems, a play, etc. [Ed.]

this style in an extract from the oration by the Archimandrite Kirill Florinsky on the birthday of the Empress Elizabeth (18 December 1741):

А врагъ всѣ́явый таковы́хъ плевелоплóдцовъ, той есть дiáволъ, котóрый до дне́шнихъ дней въ покóи уже́ небéснѣмъ ны́нѣ торже́ствующiя и́стинно благочести́вѣйшiя Екатери́ны Самоде́ржицы Всероссíйскiя утáевалъ, и хитрокóзненно скрывáлъ, тестаме́нтъ, въ немъ же тáко: О крáйняго и верьхóвнѣйшаго твоегó благополýчiя досéлѣ скрывáемаго отъ óчiю твоéю Россíе! изображенó и запечатлѣнó, по смéрти Петрá вели́каго самодержáвствовати въ Россíи благовѣ́рной Государы́нѣ Вели́кой Цесáревнѣ, я́же съ Христóмъ уже́, и́згнана отъ отéчества своегó, въ небéснѣмъ отéчествiи цáрствуетъ, Аннѣ Петрóвнѣ съ свои́ми десценде́нтами...

[This oration, delivered soon after the coup d'état which deposed Ivan VI and placed Elizabeth on the throne, is propaganda aimed at establishing the Empress's nephew (later Peter III), the orphaned child of Peter the Great's elder daughter Anna and the Duke of Holstein, as legitimate heir after Elizabeth's death. The meaning appears to be:]

And the enemy who has sown such weeds is the Devil, who until this day has kept secret and deceitfully concealed the testament of [our] truly most devout Catherine Autocrat of all Russia [i.e. Catherine I] [who is] now triumphant in heavenly rest, which [testament] says thus: O Russia! How great is your extreme and most supreme blessedness, until now concealed from your eyes! It has been set out and sealed [that] the pious Lady and Great Empress Anna Petrovna and her descendants, who, having been driven out from her fatherland, now reigns with Christ in the heavenly home, is after the death of Peter the Great to reign as autocrat in Russia...

This is the language of a dying, backward-looking literature. But now there existed another type of literature which was growing and gradually winning popularity, a literature with secular content, rich in themes of love and adventure. This new literature helped to break down the old literary language by dissolving its bookish elements in the vernacular, and at the same time ornamenting the vernacular by the introduction of fashionable western European expressions. A typical work of this kind is *Гистóрiя о россíйскомъ матрóсѣ Васи́лiи Корióтскомъ и о прекрáсной королéвнѣ Ирáклiи Флорéнской земли́*. The peculiarities of the language of this tale can be appreciated even in the following short extract:

Мину́вшу же дни по утру́ рáно прибѣжáлъ отъ мóря есаýлъ ихъ комáнды и объяви́лъ: «Господи́нъ атамáнъ, извóль командировáть пáртiю молодцóвъ на мóре, понéже по мóрю ѣ́дутъ галéры купéцкiя съ товáры». Слы́шавъ то, атамáнъ закричáлъ: «Во фрунтъ!» То во еди́ну часá мину́ту всѣ вооружи́шася и стáша во фрунтъ.

Towards a single Russian language

A day having passed, early in the morning an officer of their crew came running from the sea and announced: 'My lord ataman, pray order a party of men to put to sea, because some merchant galleys with cargo are passing.' The ataman hearing this shouted, 'Fall in!', and in one minute (of time) they all armed themselves and fell in.

This is the colloquial language of the beginning of the 18th century, in which such words and expressions as командировать, партия, во фрунт were already in common use even if they still retained a certain flavour of fashionable novelty. At the same time, however, this colloquial language contains an admixture of bookish elements which are not fully integrated with it. The most obvious archaisms are the dative absolute (минувшу же дни) and the aorist (воору-жишася, сташа). Понеже comes from the old chancellery language, and this is probably also the source of the form of the instrumental plural съ товары, which had once been normal, but by the beginning of the 18th century was already functioning as a Slavonicism. Thus the language of the courtly adventure tale, which is one of the new transitional features in literature, represents the breakdown of the former literary language, with a spontaneous tendency towards the mixing of heterogeneous linguistic material. The voluminous *История о Александре, российском дворянине* provides typical examples of this curious romantic style, as for instance in this dialogue between the hero and heroine:

Тогда Александръ обрадовался сердцемъ і не могъ долее терпети просилъ в собливую полату і говорил сице: «Дивлюся вамъ, государыня моя, что медикаментовъ не употребляешь, а внутреннеи болезни такь искусна ісцеляти, якоже свидетелствуюсь, что ни под солнцом не имеется такоі дохтурь, никакими мидикаменты возмогль бы такую неисцелимую болезнъ такь скоро сокрушить, якоже ты со мною во единъ маментъ часа улучила! коеи чести тя подобну удостою? і как могу за такое твое великое милосердие услужити, еи не дознаюсь! разве повелишь мне корету свою вместо коней возитъ? разве темъ заслужу?» Элеонора усмехьнуласъ Александрову шпынству і отвещала: «не дивис, Александре, скорому изцелению, — еще бо не имашъ прямои надежды ко здравию притти, разве будешь до 3 часа пополуночи беспокоиствовать і по окончани того ко мне чрезъ заднее крылцо придешь? обещаюсь ти написати резептъ, чрезъ которо конечно можешь болезни свободитися і паче прежняго здравие получить!»

Then Alexander rejoiced in his heart, and being unable [могъ here is a participle, cf. могши] to be patient any longer invited [her] into his own palace and spoke thus: 'I marvel at you, my lady, that you employ no medicaments, yet are so artful in curing internal ailments, as I bear witness that there is no doctor under the sun who could [возмогль is a participle] by means of any medicaments overcome an incurable illness so quickly as you managed in a single moment (of time)! What honour can I consider you fit for? (and) how I can serve you in return for such great charity I swear I know not! Perhaps you will command me to pull your carriage instead of the horses? Perhaps I can repay you in this way?' Eleanora laughed at Alexander's fancies and answered: 'Do not be astonished, Alexander, by your speedy cure, for you still have no guarantee of returning to health unless you remain awake until three in the morning and then come to me by the back door. I promise to write a prescription thanks to which you may at last be free of your illness and receive greater health than before!'

The fiction of the Petrine era is full of such phenomena giving evidence of the radical changes taking place in the written language. While it was not on this basis that the great literature of later periods grew up, this type of fiction nevertheless played an important part in the gestation of the national standard language by contributing towards the replacement of the Old Russian literary language by another in which elements of the old learned style became no more than components mixed with vernacular elements. What we are witnessing in this period, then, is the further development of processes of divergence between the two basic sources of the language, which started at a very early period (cf. the observations on the language of the *Chronicles* in chapter 6). It is clear that by the beginning of the 18th century the process which led to the modern semantic differentiation of doublets such as голова́ 'head'—глава́ 'chapter', сторона́ 'side'—страна́ 'country', неве́жа 'boor'—неве́жда 'ignoramus', горя́чий 'hot'—горя́щий 'burning', was already approaching completion. The situation still differed from that of modern Russian, however, in that it remained possible to make a purely stylistic choice between synonymous pairs such as го́род—град and отвеча́ть—отвеща́ть. We shall return to this point later. Meanwhile we must note that we have arrived at a point where changes were setting in, in the course of which the concept 'book language' (кни́жный язы́к) would cease to coincide with that of 'Church Slavonic language', and a new Russian book language would appear.

The second half of the 17th century is marked by other literary phenomena which tended to undermine further the Old Russian ecclesiastical tradition. Along with the romantic tales of love and adventure deriving from western European models, this period bequeathed to us several important literary works which clearly bear the stamp of national culture (наро́дность) and which in content and language are directly linked with folk literature. The most remarkable of these are undoubtedly the works of the archpriest Avvakum, particularly his *Life* (*Житие́*). Here is an example of his language, in which the traditional literary style is combined not with any chancellery or business language, but with that of the peasantry:

И за сіе меня боя́ринъ Васи́лѣй Петро́вичъ Шереме́тевъ, е́дучи в Каза́нь на воево́дство, в су́днѣ браня́ мно́го, и велѣ́лъ благослови́ть сы́на своего́ брадобри́тца. А́зъ же не благослови́лъ, ви́дя любодѣ́йный о́бразъ. И онъ велѣ́лъ меня́ в Во́лгу ки́нуть, и, руга́въ мно́го, столка́ли с су́дна. Та́же инъ нача́льникъ, на мя разсвирѣпѣ́въ, прiѣ́хавъ с людьми́ ко двору́ моему́, стреля́лъ из луко́въ и ис пища́лей с присту́помъ. А я в то вре́мя, заперши́ся, моли́лся ко Влады́кѣ: «Го́споди, укроти́ ево́ и примири́, ими же вѣ́си судба́ми!» Онъ же побѣжа́лъ от двора́, гони́мъ Святы́мъ Ду́хомъ. Та́же в нощь ту прибѣжа́ли от него́, зову́тъ меня́ к нему́ со слеза́ми: «ба́тюшко-госуда́рь! Евѳи́мей Стеѳа́новичь при кончи́нѣ и кричи́тъ не удо́бно, бьётъ себя́ и о́хаетъ, а самъ говори́тъ — да́йте ба́тька Авваку́ма! за него́ меня́ Богъ наказу́етъ!» И я ча́ялъ, обма́нываютъ меня́; ужа́сеся духъ мой во мнѣ. А се помоли́лъ Бо́га си́це: «Ты, Го́споди, изве́дый мя из чре́ва ма́тере моея́ и отъ небытiя́ в бытiе́ мя устро́илъ! А а́ще меня́ заду́шатъ, причти́ мя с митрополи́томъ Фили́ппомъ моско́вскимъ; а́ще ли зарѣ́жутъ, и Ты, Го́споди, причти́ мя з Заха́рiею проро́комъ; а́ще ли посадя́тъ в во́ду, и Ты Влады́ко, я́ко и Стеѳа́на Пе́рмскаго па́ки свободи́ши мя!» И моля́сь, поѣ́халъ в домъ к нему́ Евѳи́мiю. Егда́ же привезо́ша мя на дворъ, вы́бѣжала жена́ ево́ Неони́ла ухвати́ла меня́ по́д руку а сама́ говори́тъ: «поди́-тко, госуда́рь нашъ ба́тюшко, поди́-тко всѣ́тъ нашъ корми́лецъ!» И я сопроти́въ: «чю́дно! да́веча былъ бля́динъ, а топе́рьва: ба́тюшко ми́ленькой. Большо́ у Христа́-тово остра́ шелѣпуга́та: ско́ро повини́лся мужъ твой!» Ввела́ меня́ в го́рницу, вскочи́л с пери́ны Евѳи́мей, палъ пред нога́ма мои́ма, вопи́тъ неизрече́нно: «прости́, госуда́рь, согрѣши́лъ пред Бо́гомъ и пред тобо́ю!» А самъ дрожи́тъ весь. И я ему́ сопроти́во: «хо́щеши ли впредь цѣлъ бы́ти?» Онъ же лёжа отвѣща́лъ: «ей, чѣстный о́тче!». И я реклъ: «воста́ни! Богъ прости́тъ тя!» Онъ же, нака́занъ гора́здно, не могъ самъ воста́ти. И я по́днялъ, и положи́лъ ево́ на постѣ́лю, и исповѣ́далъ и ма́сломъ свяще́ннымъ пома́заль; и бысть здравъ.

And then the boyar Vasiliy Petrovich Sheremetev, on his way to take up military command in Kazan', upbraiding me greatly on the boat, ordered me to give a blessing to his shaven-chinned son. But I would not bless him, seeing his shameless face. [The Orthodox church forbade the shaving of the face. Ed.] And he commanded that I should be thrown into the Volga, so cursing me roundly they threw me off the ship... Then a certain officer who had become angry with me, coming to my house with his men, made an attack on it, shooting with bows and guns. I had locked myself in and prayed to the Lord: 'Lord, subdue him and pacify him, by those means thou knowest.' And he fled from the house pursued by the Holy Ghost. Then that night men came running from him and entreated me with tears to come to him [saying]: 'My lord priest, Yevfimey Stefanovich is at death's door and is calling out terribly, beating his breast and groaning, and he says: bring Father Avvakum, God is punishing me because of him!' And I thought they were deceiving me, and my spirit was terrified in me. So I prayed thus to God: 'Thou, Lord, who hast delivered me from my mother's womb and has brought me from non-existence to existence! If they strangle me grant me a place with Bishop Philip of Moscow, or if they slay me, then, Lord, give me a place with Zacharias the Prophet, or if they put me in the water, then, Lord, set me free again like St Stephen of Perm'.' And praying thus I set off to see him, Yevfimey, at his house. When they brought me to the courtyard his wife Neonila ran out and grasped my arm and said, 'Come, reverend Father, come, our light and our life!' But I replied, 'Very strange! Not long ago I was the son of a whore, and now I am "dear Father". The scourge of Christ is surely very sharp: your husband has admitted his guilt very quickly!' She led me into the chamber, and Yevfimey jumped from his bed and fell at my feet screaming in an inexpressible way: 'Forgive me, lord, I have sinned before God and thee.' And he was all a-tremble. So I said to him, 'Do you wish to be fit in future?' And he, lying on the ground, answered: 'I swear it, reverend Father!' So I said, 'Arise! God will forgive you!' But he was greatly afflicted and could not rise himself. So I lifted him and laid him on the bed, and heard his confession and anointed him with holy oil, and he became well.

Here the bookish element is restricted to quotations and ritual formulae, where it is undoubtedly prompted not by literary intention, but by Avvakum's professional habits. [The Church Slavonicisms in question include e.g. the aorist forms ужасеся, приведоша, бысть; the dual ногама моима; the spellings нощь, хощеши, отвещалъ; and such words as аз, паки. Ed.] But the living idiomatic Russian in which for the most part this book is written, was not yet to gain literary status for a long time to come. The way towards its acceptance was roundabout and complicated, and written Russian in the 18th century was obliged first to adapt itself to those tasks which the literature of Russian Classicism demanded of it.

9

THE LITERARY LANGUAGE OF THE AGE
OF CLASSICISM

The beginning of the period of Classicism in Russian literature is marked by the struggle between two opposing tendencies. The first found expression in the work of Trediakovsky, a fine philologist and theorist, but a poor poet. The second tendency was expressed in the work of Lomonosov, one of Russia's men of genius. So far as the Russian literary language was concerned Trediakovsky made an abortive attempt to steer it on a course towards full identification with the everyday language of the 'best society', while Lomonosov succeeded in founding a tradition of separation of the literary and everyday languages in varying degrees, dependent on the genre of the work in hand.

Lomonosov's success demonstrates how shrewdly he divined what the fundamental line for the historical development of the Russian literary language must be...It was Lomonosov who established as canonical the view that the Russian literary language was a product of the blending of the 'Slavonic' and 'Russian' sources, whereas it seemed to the young Trediakovsky that the former could be discarded completely. In the introduction to his translation of the French novel *Le Voyage de l'Isle d'Amour* by Paul Tallemant (1730), Trediakovsky assures the reader that he has translated this novel not into 'Slavonic', but 'into almost the simplest Russian, the kind we speak among ourselves'. Indeed everyday words and expressions do crop up in this book, for example бѣжа́лъ все гру́нью да́же до одного́ мѣстѣчка 'ran at full speed as far as a certain place' (гру́нью strictly means 'at a trot'), вздѣть убо́ръ 'to put on one's finery', присовѣ́товалъ чтобъ поити́ть въ оди́нъ го́родъ 'advised [him?] to go from thence to a certain town', etc. But the colloquial element in this novel is far less marked than it is, for example, in the stories about Vasiliy Koriotsky and Alexander the nobleman mentioned above. Even a brief extract will suffice to demonstrate the general features of the language Trediakovsky chose for his translation:

Мо́жетъ быть, любе́зныи мои ЛІЦІДА, что вы нема́ло ны́нѣ удивля́етеся, для того́ что я сіе́ вамъ объявля́ю надча́яніе ва́ше; но вы имѣ́ете позна́ть то, что мнѣ къ премѣ́нѣ сеи моего́ нра́ва по́дало прічі́ну увѣдомля́яся чрезъ сіе́ писмо́ о мои́хъ вторы́хъ похожде́ніяхъ, кото́рыя пои́стиннѣ бо́льше васъ имѣ́ют увесели́ть, не́жели какъ пе́рвыя. И хотя́ я ны́нѣ весма́ немы́шлю о любви́, одна́ко я вамъ признава́юсь, что о́чюнь мнѣ охо́тно жела́ется сказа́ть вамъ гісто́рію о мое́и стра́сти прешѣ́дшеи.

It may be, my dear Lycidas, that you are now no little surprised that I make public to you this your intention(?) but you must know what it was that gave rise to this change in my character, by learning from this letter about my second [series of] adventures, which must certainly entertain you even more than the first. And although at the present time I have no thought whatever for love, yet I confess to you that I desire very greatly to tell you the history of my late passion.

One can scarcely believe that even an 'illustrious society' (изря́дная компа́ния) would use such turgid officialese for their everyday speech. It is obvious that Trediakovsky was trying to transfer wholesale into Russian the linguistic conventions which he had observed in France. He thought that just as France had the language of the Versailles court, so in Russia there must exist a language of élite circles distinguished by an elegant austerity and purity which could serve as the model for the literary language. Hence Trediakovsky's doctrine of the 'best usage' (лу́чшее употребле́ние) borrowed from such French theorists as Vaugelas, the author of the well-known *Remarques sur la langue française, utiles à ceux qui veulent bien parler et bien escrire*, 1647. According to Vaugelas, the language the majority of people used was bad, while that of court circles and the best contemporary authors was good. All this was very far from the realities which Trediakovsky must have found on his return from Paris to Russia. Obviously in the first half of the 18th century in Russia the everyday language, even that of court society (which never at any time was a cultural avant-garde) did not possess qualities which, reproduced as they stood, could solve the problem of the literary language. Rather the reverse: in this respect it was society that would have to expect guidance from literature, and not literature from society...

And when the necessary conditions for this came about, what Trediakovsky had failed to do was achieved with phenomenal success at the end of the century by the school of Karamzin. This success was the result of the lessons learned in the period between

Trediakovsky's time and that of Karamzin, the period of Classicism. The most important point to note in the ideas of the Russian Classicists concerning language, as they are expressed in the works of Lomonosov and other writers, is that they acknowledge the essential core of 'Slavo-Russian' (славенороссійскій) in the Russian literary language. According to this view, the language of ecclesiastical books and the Russian language have much in common, and even coincide to some extent, and it is this common material from both styles which provides the starting point for the Russian literary language. In the course of their writing, authors would add elements sometimes from the purely 'Slavonic', sometimes from the purely 'Russian' sources, depending on the circumstances. These additions had tremendous practical significance for solving specific literary problems, since they created the linguistic basis for 'high' and 'low' genres, allowing the language of odes and tragedies to be distinguished from that of fables and comedies.

The creation of the high and low styles, however, while it was of great direct importance in the field of literature, had only an indirect effect on the literary language itself. It opened up the way for the development of the so-called 'middle style', which was intended primarily not for literature, but for scientific and journalistic writings: that is, for exactly the kind of writings in which the process of blending the learned and everyday languages into an integrated standard literary language could proceed most successfully. One need make only a cursory comparison of the three basic styles of language in the literature of the Age of Classicism to be convinced that the growing point of literary Russian lay entirely in the middle style, whatever may have been the merits of the other two styles within the existing literary framework. Here is a typical example of high style:

> Князь Курбскій возопилъ, алкая с нимъ схватиться:
> Не стыдно ль множеству съ единымъ купно биться?
> Храните рыцарскій, герои, в бранѣхъ чинъ;
> Оставьте насъ, хощу съ нимъ ратовать единъ.
> Услышавъ Гидромиръ отважну рѣчь толику,
> Висящу вдоль бедры взялъ палицу велику;
> Онъ ею въ воздухѣ полкруга учинилъ,
> Часть Муромскихъ дворянъ на землю преклонилъ.
> И князя бъ разразилъ шумящей булавою,
> Но онъ къ главѣ коня приникъ своей главою,
> И тако угонзнулъ[1] не поврежденъ ни чѣмъ;

[1] угонзнулъ 'escaped'.

Но Гидроми́ра въ пахъ пора́нилъ онъ мече́мъ,
Разсвире́пѣлъ злодѣй, болѣнію не внѣмлетъ,
Какъ ма́чту па́лицу тяжёлую подъе́млетъ,
И Му́ромскихъ дворя́нъ, и Ку́рбскаго рази́тъ,
Тамъ шле́мы сокруши́лъ, тамъ ла́ты, та́мо щитъ.

This is from Kheraskov's *Россия́да.*

Our example of simple or low style is taken from Sumarokov's comedy *Опеку́н* (*The Guardian*):

Намня́сь[1] ви́дѣлъ я, какъ че́стной-то по ва́шему и безче́стной, а по мо́ему разу́мной и безу́мной принима́лися. Безче́стной-атъ, по ва́шему, приѣхалъ, такъ ему́ стулъ, да ещё въ хоро́шенькомъ до́мѣ: все ли въ до́бромъ здоро́вьи? какова́ твоя́ хозя́юшка? дѣтки? Что такъ запалъ?[2] ни къ намъ не жа́луешь, ни къ себѣ не зовёшь; а всѣ вѣ́даютъ то, что онъ чужи́мъ и непра́веднымъ разжи́лся. А че́стнова-та человѣ́ка дѣтки пришли́ ми́лостины проси́ть, кото́рыхъ оте́цъ ѣ́здилъ до Кита́йчетава ца́рства и былъ во Камча́тномъ госуда́рствѣ, и объ е́томъ госуда́рствѣ написа́лъ по́вѣсть; одна́ко ска́зку то ево́ чита́ютъ, а дѣтки то ево́ хо́дятъ по́ міру; а у до́чекъ то ево́ крашени́нныя бостроки,[3] да и тѣ въ запла́тахъ.

Since the works in the middle style are more varied in genre, two examples are given below. One comes from the periodical *Вся́кая Вся́чина* (*All Manner of Things*), 1769:

Вельмо́жа оди́нъ приговори́лъ ко сме́рти одного́ своего́ нево́льника, кото́рый не ви́дя уже́ наде́жды ко спасе́нію своего́ живота́, зача́лъ брани́ть и проклина́ть вельмо́жу. Сей не разумѣ́я языка́ нево́льнича, спроси́лъ у о́коло стоя́щихъ свои́хъ дома́шнихъ: что нево́льникъ говори́тъ? Оди́нъ вы́звался, говоря́: госуда́рь, сей безща́стный ска́зываетъ, чай[4] рай приуго́товленъ для тѣхъ, кои уменьша́ютъ свой гнѣвъ, и проща́ютъ преступле́нія. Вельмо́жа прости́лъ нево́льника. Други́й изъ бли́жнихъ его́ вскрича́лъ: не присто́йно лгать пе́редъ Его́ Сія́тельствомъ, и поверни́ся къ лицу́ вельмо́жи сказа́лъ: сей престу́пникъ васъ проклина́етъ вели́кими кля́твами, мой това́рищъ вамъ объяви́лъ ложь непрости́тельную. Вельмо́жа отвѣ́тствовалъ: ста́ться мо́жетъ; но его́ ложь есть человѣколюби́вѣе, не́жели твоя́ пра́вда; и́бо онъ иска́лъ спасти́ человѣ́ка, а ты стара́ешься двухъ погуби́ть.

The other is from one of the works compiled by the translator Vasiliy Levshin, *Чудеса́ нату́ры или собра́ніе необыкнове́нныхъ и примѣча́нія досто́йныхъ явле́ній и приключе́ніи въ цѣ́ломъ мі́рѣ тѣлъ* (1788):

Въ 1779 году́ пока́зывали въ Пари́жской Акаде́міи Нау́къ сохраня́емую въ спи́ртѣ я́щерицу съ двумя́ голова́ми, и обнадёживали, по свидѣ́тельству вѣроя́тія досто́йныхъ осо́бъ, что э́та тварь въ жи́зни свое́й обѣ́ими голова́ми дѣла́ свои́ исправля́ла; она́ ѣла обо́ими рта́ми, и смотрѣ́ла всѣ́ми четырмя́ глаза́ми. Особли́вѣйшее обстоя́тельство при томъ бы́ло сіе́, что когда́

---

[1] намнясь 'the other day'.   [2] запаль 'disappeared'.
[3] бострокъ kind of coat.   [4] чай 'no doubt'.

клáли хлѣбъ съ обѣихъ сторóнъ таковы́мъ óбразомъ, чтобъ я́щерица находя́щійся съ прáвой стороны́ кусóкъ ви́дѣла тóлько прáвымъ глáзомъ прáвой головы́, а на лѣвой сторонѣ тóлько лѣвымъ глáзомъ лѣвой стороны́; слѣдовала онá закóнамъ равновѣсія, не такъ какъ Буридáновъ осёлъ терпѣлъ въ семъ слýчаѣ гóлодъ, но дви́галась пря́мо впередъ до тѣхъ поръ, какъ движéніе э́то закрывáло видъ хлѣба у однóй головы́, тогдá ужé шла онá пря́мо къ одномý кускý.

Bearing in mind that this is a translation, the briefest comparison with the examples from translated texts of the time of Peter I quoted above will show the tremendous strides made by the Russian national standard language in its written form in the course of the 18th century. These two last-quoted extracts are written in a language which differs from the Russian of the 19th and 20th centuries only in very minor ways: in the first extract there is живóтъ with the meaning of жизнь, зачáлъ instead of нáчалъ, поверня́ся instead of повернýвшись; in the second it is mainly in syntax that the language does not coincide with contemporary Russian. One feels that the learned and colloquial sides have already come into a state of equilibrium, in the sense that they are participating as members enjoying equal rights in the same linguistic system, liberated from their stylistic doublets and parallels. By the end of the 18th century, if people writing in the middle style used the word гóлодъ, then they did not use гладъ, and if they used надéжда, then they did not use надéжа, and so on, while the words странá and сторонá were used only with different meanings. Naturally this is not a hard and fast rule without exceptions, but it is a general tendency. Thus towards the end of the 18th century the process of mutual demarcation of 'Slavonic' and Russian elements on the one hand, and on the other their fusion into a single whole, may be considered as complete.

Lomonosov's *Россійская Граммáтика* (1755) makes this process particularly clear. The composition of this grammar is Lomonosov's chief claim to recognition as a great figure in the history of the Russian language. His is the first grammar of Russian in Russian. It was only with its appearance that the re-issues of Smotritsky began to be ousted from the classroom, and people began to accustom themselves to the idea, later supported, for instance, by Radishchev, that primary instruction should be given in Russian and not in Church Slavonic. At the same time Lomonosov's is not, of course, a grammar of the everyday language 'of simple conversation'. It reflects the norms of the new learned language as it was taking shape in the tradition of the 'middle style', based on the fusion of the 'Slavonic' and 'Russian' elements into one whole. In this respect it is noteworthy that Lomonosov in his *Grammar* attacks certain forms generally accepted in his day, which were in opposition to his basic conception of the Russian literary language.

For instance, Lomonosov protests against the use of the [nominative plural] forms учрежденіи instead of учрежденія and истинныи извѣстіи instead of истинныя извѣстія, that is against forms prompted by everyday speech habits. But at the same time he scarcely includes in his *Grammar* a single form which in his time would have been felt to be a Slavonicism, such as the simple past tenses, or archaic forms of the masculine declension in the plural (рабомъ, рабы, рабѣхъ, etc.). It is extremely interesting to find how wholeheartedly Trediakovsky concurred with him in his views on grammar, which also represent the middle line of development of the new written language. Thus, on the one hand Trediakovsky joins Lomonosov in condemning such colloquial forms as pacyжденіи, повелѣніи instead of pacyжденія, повелѣнія (nominative plural), прімѣчаніевъ, склоненіевъ instead of прімѣчаній, склоненій (genitive plural), and on the other hand objects to the use of such archaisms as по торгомъ і рынкомъ (dative plural) or въ рядѣхъ і на плошчадѣхъ (locative plural) instead of по торгамъ і рынкамъ and въ рядахъ і на плошчадяхъ.

Characteristically, however, the language of literature in the 18th century lagged behind this process. The reason for this is clear: Russian Classicism recognised as proper to literature primarily the 'high' and 'low' genres. The 'high' genres forced the writer to resort to bookish forms which had already been discarded by the main stream of development of the literary language. (An analogous situation could be seen in the lower genres in respect of the vernacular.) Therefore an 18th-century ode or tragedy tends towards Biblical turgidity, while a comedy or fable smacks of 'vulgar speech' (простонаро́дность) and provincialism. The writers of odes loved flowery Hellenisms such as елéй 'oil', кринъ 'lily', нектáръ 'nectar', понтъ 'sea' (esp. Black Sea), compound words of Hellenistic style such as быстротекýщій 'swift flowing', огнедышущий 'firebreathing', злосéрдый 'malicious', златострýнный 'silver-stringed', свѣтоно́сный 'radiant'. They chose high-flown words and expressions from the language of ecclesiastical books, such as воспящáть 'turn back', вперйть 'direct', вотщé 'in vain', ложеснá 'womb', лѣпотá 'beauty', помавáть 'wave', стóгна 'city square', угобзйть 'multiply', ликовствовать 'rejoice' and also words which had a different meaning in the ordinary language, for example живóтъ in the meaning 'life', instead of 'belly' (e.g. Sumarokov has: И во злóбѣ устремлéнныхъ на драгóй живóтъ Петрóвъ 'And in anger turned upon Peter's cherished life'), текý in the meaning 'go, move', instead of 'flow' (e.g. V. Petrov has: Герóйства Россъ на пóдвигъ текъ 'The Russian advanced to a feat of arms'), хребетъ in the meaning 'back' instead of 'spine' (e.g. Kapnist has: я зрю васъ, устрашéнныхъ и обращáющихъ хребéтъ 'I see you, turning your backs in fear'), etc. One feature of this style is its preference for archaic variants of verb stems in compounds, e.g. снити, внити for сойтй 'descend', войтй 'enter'; пожерти, стерти for пожрáть 'devour', стерéть 'rub off', предписовати, испытовати (present tense предписýю, испытýю), for предпйсывать, испы́тывать, and in particular its preference for archaic forms of the present tense, such as зижду, from здать 'build', éмлю from имáть 'take', женý from гнать 'drive' (compare e.g. Kheraskov's *Россияда*: Четы́ре хрáбрые герóя ихъ женýтъ 'The four brave heroes pursue them'). It also favoured archaic forms of participles such as сѣдяй (сидя́щий), создавый (создáвший), явльшійся (явйвшийся), and many other grammatical and lexical peculiarities. In the sphere of pronunciation the evidence available indicates the continuation during the 18th century of the tradition of elevated learned pronunciation, which did not allow аканье, tried to make an artificial distinction between ѣ and е, and considered the pronunciation of г as a plosive [g] uneducated, demanding that it should be the fricative [γ]. Similarly the use of ё was not permitted, as we see in such rhymes as чѣмъ—мечéмъ (i.e. мечóм), дѣла—сéла (сёла), пещéръ—озéръ (озёр).

Lomonosov's odes and other high-style works are considerably simpler in their language than subsequent works in the Classical tradition which he established. His contemporaries and rivals frequently reproached him for his excessively grandiose images and exaggerated comparisons, but on the whole these faults cannot be attached to his language. Many passages in Sumarokov's tragedies, Kheraskov's *Россияда*, Maykov's odes, and in particular V. Petrov's odes, are written in a language far more elaborate, difficult and full of Biblical phrases, than Lomonosov's.

In general, then, the tradition of high style which had become established caused difficulties, especially for writers of prose, because of its total detachment from 'ordinary' language. In this respect Fonvizin's introduction to [the once-famous poem] *Joseph* by Paul Jérémie Bitaubé, which he translated in 1769, is of great interest. Here is what he says about the language of his translation:

Всѣ на́ши кни́ги пи́саны и́ли славе́нскимъ, и́ли ны́нѣшнимъ языко́мъ. Мо́жет быть, я ошиба́юсь, но мнѣ ка́жется, что въ перево́дѣ таки́хъ книгъ, како́въ Телема́къ, Аргени́да, Іо́сифъ и про́чія сего́ ро́да, потре́бно держа́ться то́кмо ва́жности славе́нскаго языка́: но при томъ наблюда́ть и я́сность на́шего; и́бо хотя́ славе́нскій язы́къ и самъ собо́ю я́сенъ, но не для тѣхъ, ко́и въ немъ не упражня́ются. Слѣ́довательно слогъ до́лженъ быть тако́й, какова́го мы ещё не имѣ́емъ... Мно́жество приходи́ло мнѣ на мысль славе́нскихъ слов́ъ и рече́ній, кото́рыя, не имѣ́я себѣ́ примѣ́ра, принужде́нъ я былъ оста́вить, боя́ся и́ли возмути́ть я́сность, и́ли тро́нуть нѣ́жность слу́ха. Приходи́ли мнѣ на мысль на́ши ны́нѣшнія слова́ и рече́нія, и весьма́ употреби́тельныя въ сообще́ствѣ, но не имѣ́я примѣ́ру, оставля́лъ я о́ныя,[1] опаса́ясь того́, что не дово́льно изобразя́тъ они́ ва́жность а́вторской мы́сли.

This expresses very accurately the need that was felt in Russian literature for a language which, on the one hand, would not be so trivial and familiar as everyday speech, but, on the other, would not be so elevated and learned that it presented too marked a contrast with the vernacular.

It is quite natural that this demand was met earlier in prose than in verse. Quite apart from the fact that exalted poetry understandably required elevated diction to a much greater extent than prose, there existed another peculiar circumstance which caused poetic language in general to lag behind in the general evolution of the Russian literary language towards a closer relationship with everyday speech. From the very birth of Russian poetry at the end of the 17th and beginning of the 18th centuries the lack of an established tradition and techniques forced the poets to resort to various 'poetic licences' in order to be able to cope with the demands of rhythm and rhyme. It is not a question of occasional deviations from the norm by individual writers, but of a whole system of poetic diction legitimised not only by tradition but by specific theoretical arguments, consisting in the main of the acceptance of archaisms and other linguistic variants. Particularly important in this respect was the role of morphological

---

[1] оныя 'those'.

Slavonicisms, which differed from the analogous words in the ordinary language by being shorter or longer by one syllable. They were therefore useful among the stock-in-trade of the versifier, e.g. всякъ instead of всякій, Петре (vocative) instead of Петръ, писати instead of писать, моръ instead of морéй, etc. The same feature appeared in certain lexical variants, e.g. иль instead of или, градъ instead of городъ, etc. Antiokh Kantemir wrote about this question as follows: Все сокращéнія рѣчéй, котóрыя славéнскій язы́къ узаконя́етъ, мóжно по нуждѣ смѣло приня́ть въ стихáхъ рýсскихъ; такъ, напримѣръ, изря́дно употребля́ется *вѣкъ, человѣкъ, чистъ, сладкъ,* вмѣсто *вѣкóвъ, человѣковъ, чи́стый, слáдкій.* Naturally, resort was made to such 'liberties' (i.e. to various archaisms justified not only on stylistic but on technical grounds) in both elevated and low-style poetry. In the following fable by Sumarokov, for instance, It is easy to detect a number of such shortened and lengthened words:

СТРЕКАЗА

Въ зи́мнѣ врéмя, подая́нья
Прóситъ жáлко стреказá,
И заплáканны глазá,
Тяжковá ея́ страдáнья,
Представля́ютъ видъ.
Муравéйникъ посѣщáетъ,
Лю́ту гóресть извѣщáетъ,
        Говори́тъ:
    — Стрáжду;
Сжáлься, сжáлься муравéй,
Ты надъ бѣдностью моéй,
Утоли́ мой алчь и жáжду!
Рáзны мýки я терплю́:
        Гóлодъ,
        Хóлодъ;
День таскáюсь, ночь не сплю.
    — Въ чемъ труди́лася ты въ лѣто?
    — Я скажý тебѣ и éто:
Я вспѣвáла день и ночь.
    — Коль такóе вáше плéмя;
Так лети́ отсéль ты прочь:
Попляса́ти врéмя.

[The shortened forms include зи́мнѣ for зи́мнее, заплáканны for заплáканные, and лю́ту for лю́тую; and the lengthenings труди́лася for труди́лась, вспѣвáла for пѣла; тяжковá has lengthened stem but shortened ending—тя́жкія, neuter plural.]
The tradition of 'liberties' (вóльности) persisted for a very long

time, and it was only in the middle of the 19th century, after Pushkin's time, that it finally died out.

The language of the low genres also lagged behind in its own way. By the end of the 18th century it must already have sounded vulgar, coarse and provincial. One constantly comes across such words and phrases as стибрить 'steal', подтяпать 'undercut', калякатъ 'chat', кобéниться 'be contorted', дать стрѣлка́ 'run away', заварить брáгу 'have a spree', остáться въ гóляхъ 'to lose by something', and кто бáбѣ не внукъ 'everybody has a grandmother'. It contained many words which are now to be found only in specialised dialect dictionaries, such as куромша 'unreliable person' (вéтреник), набитóй братъ 'one's equal' (рóвня), похи́мистить 'steal' (украсть), взáбыль 'in fact' (в сáмом дéле), врютить 'involve' (впутать), притомáнное 'earned' (зарабóтанное). The *Запи́ски* by Bolotov[1] are a fascinating example of the 'low' style, and to a considerable extent appear to reflect the speech of the author, his times and his milieu. He uses such expressions as узгъ топорá 'edge of an axe', промолóл я её всю 'I learned the whole book', подъ караýлъ подтя́пали 'whisked him off under arrest', скóлько-нибудь понаблóшнился и мнóго кое-чего зналъ 'picked up [literally 'fleas'] a certain amount and knew quite a lot', покýда онъ ещё не оборкáлся 'until he got used to it', кóлты и хлóпоты 'troubles and bother', слѣ́довалъ за нáми нази́ркою до сáмого Рéвеля 'watched us like a hawk all the way to Revel'', женá егó былá старýшка сáмая шлю́шечка 'his wife was a real old bag', бýде бы онъ сталъ сли́шкомъ барабóшить 'as if he had argued too much', óколо замкá шишля́ю 'I am fumbling away with the lock'. Along with these items of vocabulary go such grammatical peculiarities as the postpositive particles -атъ, -сте, -стани [cf. the passage from Sumarokov on p. 100; and e.g. from M. Matinsky's comedy *Санктпетербýргской Гости́ной дворъ* (1791): Пожáлуй-сте къ намъ 'Do come in to visit us'], declensional forms like сто рублёвъ [instead of рублéй], три дни [дня], изъ стремя [стрéмени], яйцы [яйца], укрепленьевъ [укреплéний], many verbs with the suffix -ыва- such as ночёвывалъ 'used to spend the night', кýпывались 'used to bathe', ýжинывалъ 'used to have supper', etc. This was the everyday speech of a society which did not yet possess a standard language as a normal part of its everyday life.

[1] A. T. Bolotov (1738–1833), one of the first Russian writers on agriculture. [Ed.]

Literary language of the Age of Classicism

We have traced above the main essentials of the state of the Russian literary language of the Age of Classicism. Its development up to the last two decades of the 18th century can be summed up in two basic statements:

(1) The concept of a national standard language had been consolidated on the basis of the middle style, which represented an advance in the process of blending the learned and everyday language sources. But so far this concept remained restricted in practice to business or technical writing (scientific, journalistic, etc.) and had little contact with literature proper.

(2) Classicism had achieved an excellent solution to the problem of language at this stage in the development of Russian literature, by creating the conventions of high and low styles. But as time went on an ever-increasing contradiction manifested itself between the general line of development of the written language, and its manifestation in the basic literary genres, in which the language was constantly being felt to be either too 'high' or too 'low'.

The two contradictions indicated above were destined to be resolved by the new era in the history of Russian literature instituted by Karamzin.

10

THE CREATION OF THE NATIONAL
STANDARD LANGUAGE

The natural way to eliminate the contradictions mentioned above was to make the language which had grown up on the basis of the middle style not only the language of business and science, but also of literature. This in essence was what Karamzin did in his 'reform of style', which produced such profound repercussions in Russian society at the end of the 18th and the beginning of the 19th centuries. But this reform became possible only when literature itself had changed and had begun to set itself new tasks. Thus the struggle which took place between старым и новым слогом российского языка at the end of the 18th century was the direct consequence of the struggle between Classicism in literature and the new trend which later was unfortunately called Sentimentalism. In his article of 1803 *От чего в России мало авторских талантов*, Karamzin said, amongst other things, that Russian authors, in contrast to French writers, were deprived of the chance of learning good language in society: obviously he shared none of the young Trediakovsky's illusions on this point. Therefore, he concludes, 'The French write as they speak, but on many subjects the Russians are still forced to speak in a way a talented person would write.' This comment was absolutely correct, not only in so far as it stated the writer's problem, but as an observation of the realities of the situation.

At the end of the 18th century there already existed vast differences between the everyday speech of the various classes which made up Russian society. Admittedly in the first decades of the 19th century certain circles of the Russian nobility still clung to the habits of 'common' (простонародный) Russian speech. We see this for example, in Griboyedov's *Горе от ума*, and in private correspondence and memoirs belonging to the time. Thus even Chatsky still says: вы ради, давиче, спосылать за делом [for вы рады, недавно, посла́ть], and Pushkin writes in his letters, пока́месть, я́рмонка, брюха́та, на кварте́ре etc. [for пока́ 'until', я́рмарка 'fair', бере́менна 'pregnant', в кварти́ре 'in the flat']. But, on the other hand, already in Fonvizin's play *Недоросль* (1782) the linguistic differentiation mentioned comes through distinctly. All we need do to see this is to compare the speech of the negative and positive characters of this comedy: the latter always speak in a bookish manner—in the language of the books which nourished their thoughts and feelings. Here is an example:

Софья. Ва́ше изъясне́ніе, дя́дюшка, схо́дно съ мои́мъ вну́треннимъ чу́вст-вомъ, кото́рова я изъясни́ть не могла́. Я тепе́рь жи́во чу́вствую и досто́инство че́стнова челове́ка, и ево́ до́лжность.

Стародумъ. До́лжность! А! Мой другъ! какъ э́то сло́во у всѣхъ на языкѣ, и какъ ма́ло ево́ понима́ютъ! Всечасное употребле́ніе э́това сло́ва такъ насъ съ нимъ ознако́мило, что вы́говоря ево́ челове́къ ничево́ уже́ не мы́слить, ничево́ не чу́вствуетъ, когда́ е́стьлибъ лю́ди понима́ли ево́ ва́жность, никто́ не могъ бы вы́молвить ево́ безъ душе́внаго почте́ніия. Поду́май, что тако́е до́лжность. Это тоть свяще́нный обѣтъ...

Here the word до́лжность signifies 'social obligation' and is one of those fashionable bookish words of this period, which, as Klyuchevsky once remarked, 'did not have any direct effect on manners and actions or on raising the cultural level of life, but which made an adornment to speech and trained us to think in an orderly way'. The style of speech to which words of this kind belonged, at the end of the 18th century became an everyday matter, a habit, for a certain section of the population. These people were the forerunners of the Russian intelligentsia, and they gradually began to use the language they read in their favourite books as their spoken language.

Apart from all the other differences between the new bookish 'middle style' Russian and previous stages in the development of the national language, it was different also in that it was a Europeanised language. We have already pointed out what a very important part translations from western European languages played in the history of Russian. In the process of translating, means had to be found for transferring the concepts of western European civilisation. This was achieved in two ways. The main category of borrowings was that of international scientific terminology derived from the Classical languages. As a result words like амфитеа́тр, атмосфе́ра, горизо́нт, инструме́нт, натура́льный, регуля́рный, пра́ктика, пропо́рция, температу́ра, тракта́т, фо́рмула etc. were absorbed into the normal

Russian vocabulary. The second way was more complicated. It consisted of translating literally the corresponding words of the foreign languages and making new Russian words—these are called 'loan translations' or 'calques'. It is very important to bear in mind that the material used for this loan translation of foreign learned vocabulary was taken exclusively from Church Slavonic. In 1752, when doubt arose about the legitimacy of the words which Trediakovsky was using in order to transmit philosophical terms accepted in the west (words like естéственность or сýщность 'essentia', разýмность 'intelligentia', чýвственность 'sensatio', etc.), Trediakovsky with justification cited the ecclesiastical language as his source. He wrote: Оныи тéрмины подтверждáются всѣ кнѝгами нáшими церкóвными, изъ котóрыхъ я óныи взялъ 'All these terms are substantiated by our ecclesiastical books, from whence I took them'. But in this way also many completely new words could be coined, words like предрассýдок 'prejudice', originally предсуждéніе or предразсуждéніе, which is built up from Church Slavonic material exactly on the model of the French 'pré-jugé'. It was in this way that Russian equivalents of many general European learned terms came into being—words such as преломлéніе 'refraction', óпыт 'experiment, experience', истолковáніе 'interpretation', and many others. The language used by Lomonosov in his scientific works was enormously important in this process. All the words of this kind which became current towards the end of the 18th century, although Russian in appearance, were essentially of general European, international origin. By this means Russian was brought into the community of modern European languages.

Hand in hand with this terminological enrichment of the written language went the process of assimilation into the spoken language of everyday words of western origin. From the time of Peter I such words had been taking root in the everyday language of the ruling classes, along with imported forms of dress, food, utensils, etc. These were words such as суп, фрýкты, сюртýк (formerly сюртýт, French 'surtout') 'coat', сервѝз 'dinner service', compare for example in the tale *Пригóжая поварѝха* by M. Chulkov: Купѝлъ мнѣ нóвой сервѝзъ, или пóпросту посýду, etc.—for, according to Pushkin:

> Но панталóны, фрак, жилéт,
> Всех э́тих слов на рýсском нет.
> (*Евгений Онегин* I, xxvi)

110

In the second half of the 18th century, however, the Russian aristocracy went through a veritable fever of imitation of things European, and particularly French, not only in external aspects of life but also in language. In certain circles of the aristocracy the superficial assimilation of French culture led to the typical phenomenon of the *petit-maître* and the dandy, whose manner of speech was repeatedly parodied in the comedies of the 18th century, and to whom Griboyedov's satirical label 'смесь французского с нижегородским'—'a mixture of French and Nizhni-Novgorod' might well be applied. In Sumarokov's comedy *Мать совмѣстница дочери,* the mother, while trying to win over her daughter's sweetheart, talks to him like this: Да неужъ ли вамъ безъ женитьбы и любить не капабельно, будто только и кариспанденціи какъ мужъ и жена! or like this: Я имѣю честь имѣти къ вашему патрету, или къ вашей персонѣ отличной решпектъ, и принимала васъ безо всякой церемоніальности и безъ фасоній. In Fonvizin's play *Бригадиръ,* Sovetnitsa says to her husband: Я капабельна съ тобою развестися, ежели ты меня ещё такъ шпетить[1] станешь. These are of course caricatures, but obviously they had counterparts in real life. That the use of western European borrowings was dictated not by the need for suitable terminology but by fashion, is easy to see in examples taken from Bolotov's *Записки* in which we come across such phrases as: выслушивать таковыя ея предики и нравоученія; онъ былъ мужъ, или паче сказать носилъ только имя мужа полковничей метресы или любовницы; дѣло, о которомъ я теперь расскажу, основалось на мошенническомъ комплотѣ или заговорѣ между чухнами; имѣвшій съ покойнымъ родителемъ моимъ...небольшую суспицію или досаду.

This Frenchified fashion was indulged in primarily by the more conservative sections of society, and not by the more progressive: not the Starodums and Pravdins, but the Ivanushkas and Sovetnitsas, but nevertheless it had its effect on the spoken Russian of the time as a whole. From the end of the century it became almost obligatory in aristocratic homes to have the children instructed in French from the outset, and the habit of speaking and reading French trained them even to think in French. In this truly bilingual atmosphere gallicisms of various kinds became current—that is turns of speech literally translated from French or constructed on the model of French

---

[1] шпетить 'insult'.

syntax. Thus they would say of children that они дѣлают зу́бки—*ils font ses dents* 'they are cutting teeth', and expressions like взять терпѣние—*prendre patience* 'have patience with' appeared. In Fonvizin's *Нѣдоросль*, Pravdin says Ра́дуюсь, сдѣлавъ Ва́ше знако́мство—*de faire votre connaissance*; instead of заплати́ть за кни́гу one heard заплати́ть кни́гу—*payer le livre*; даю́т себе́ во́здухи—*se donner des airs* 'to give oneself airs' instead of принима́ют вид; and трѣбуют when they meant утвержда́ют (French *prétendre* means both 'to claim, require' and 'to maintain, assert') and so on.

There was not a single author who encouraged this fashionable linguistic gallomania as such. On the contrary, the struggle against gallomania is a general characteristic of Russian literature throughout the 18th century, from Lomonosov to Karamzin. Occasionally it went to completely naive and touching lengths. In Lukin's comedy *Мотъ, любо́вію испра́вленный*, one of the characters uses the word туалѣ́тъ, and the author gives a footnote: Сло́во чужестра́нное говори́тъ коке́тка что для нея́ и прили́чно, а ѣ́жели бы не она́ говори́ла то коне́чно бы ру́сское бы́ло напи́сано 'It is a coquette who uses this foreign word, which is fitting for her, but if it hadn't been she who was speaking, then of course a Russian word would have been written'. This is the same Lukin who uses for the title of another of his comedies the bizarre dialect word Щепети́льникъ meaning 'haberdasher', which requires a long explanation in the foreword: this was to avoid галантере́йщик, a borrowing from French, which Lukin himself admits already existed at that time in ordinary speech.

The process of rapprochement between Russian and western European languages, however, was not entirely a matter of mere transitory fashion. The new literature which began to oust Classicism at the end of the 18th century, and which clearly reflected the transplantation of the 'middle style' from books into the everyday usage of the educated section of the upper classes, was destined to assist in selecting what was useful and essential from the stream of borrowed and Frenchified expressions which appeared at the end of the 18th and the beginning of the 19th centuries. It is in the fulfilment of this task that we must recognise the historical achievements of Russian Sentimentalism and its leader Karamzin. In his essay of 1802 *О любви́ к оте́честву и наро́дной го́рдости*, Karamzin writes among other things:

Я осме́люсь попеня́ть мно́гим из на́ших люби́телей чте́ния, кото́рые, зна́я лу́чше Пари́жских жи́телей все произведе́ния Францу́зской Литерату́ры, не хотя́т и взгляну́ть на Ру́скую кни́гу. Того́ ли они́ жела́ют, что́бы иностра́нцы уведомля́ли их о Ру́ских тала́нтах? Пусть же чита́ют Францу́зские и Неме́цкие крити́ческие Журна́лы, кото́рые отдаю́т справедли́вость на́шим дарова́ниям, су́дя по не́которым перево́дам. Кому́ не бу́дет оби́дно походи́ть на Даланбе́ртову ма́мку, кото́рая, живу́чи с ним, к изумле́нию своему́ услы́шала от други́х, что он у́мный челове́к. Не́которые извиня́ются худы́м зна́нием Ру́скаго языка́: э́то извине́ние ху́же само́й вины́. Оста́вим на́шим любе́зным све́тским Да́мам утвержда́ть, что Ру́ской язы́к груб и не прия́тен, что charmant и séduisant, expansion и vapeurs не мо́гут быть на нем вы́ражены, и что, одни́м сло́вом, не сто́ит труда́ знать его́. Кто сме́ет дока́зывать Да́мам, что они́ ошиба́ются? Но мущи́ны не име́ют тако́го любе́знаго пра́ва суди́ть ло́жно. Язы́к наш вырази́телен не то́лько для высо́каго красноре́чия, для гро́мкой, живопи́сной Поэ́зии, но и для не́жной простоты́, для зву́ков се́рдца и чувстви́тельности. Он бога́тее гармо́ниею не́жели Францу́зской, спосо́бнее для излия́ния души́ в то́нах, представля́ет бо́лее аналоги́ческих слов, то есть сообра́зных с выража́емым де́йствием: вы́года, кото́рую име́ют одни́ коренны́е языки́! Беда́ на́ша, что мы все хоти́м говори́ть по-францу́зски, и не ду́маем труди́ться над обрабо́тыванием со́бственного языка́: мудрено́ ли, что не уме́ем изъясня́ть им не́которых то́нкостей в разгово́ре...Язы́к ва́жен для Патрио́та; и я люблю́ Англича́н за то, что они́ лу́чше хотя́т *свиста́ть* и *шипе́ть* по-англи́йски с са́мыми не́жными любо́вницами свои́ми, не́жели говори́ть чужи́м языко́м, изве́стным почти́ вся́кому из них.

This excerpt, which expresses Karamzin's attitude towards the Russian language and to the problem of its literary development, at the same time characterises the very language Karamzin used himself. It was clear that his sincerely patriotic love for the language could be reconciled completely with the use in a Russian text of learned terms of western European origin and with turns of phrase in the European manner. While acknowledging the high quality of Russian speech, Karamzin calls for its refinement—'обрабо́тывание', so that it may be made an appropriate and worthy vehicle for contemporary Russian culture. This was to be a language equally suited for books or conversation—and of course suitable for the educated circle, who could read and who wanted to speak not just anyhow, but well and purely, or as we say now 'in a cultured way'—'культу́рно'. This was to be not the language used at home, but such as a man of culture used in society—a language polished and refined in conformity with literary models, but nevertheless conversational and not only suitable for academic speech and printed discourse. Karamzin did not close his eyes to the fact that in his age and circle French was already fulfilling this function, and it was precisely this function that

he was contesting. He writes: Ру́ской Кандида́т Авторства, недо-
во́льный кни́гами, до́лжен закры́ть их и слу́шать вокру́г себя́
разгово́ры, что́бы соверше́ннее узна́ть язы́к. Тут но́вая беда́: в
лу́чших дома́х говоря́т у нас бо́лее по-Францу́зски! But the ideal
language of which Karamzin dreamed was indeed intended to oust
French as the language of the educated Russian. This accounts for
the invention of new words and expressions in which Karamzin
delighted. It was he who introduced into the Russian language words
like промы́шленность, бу́дущность, разви́тие, влия́ние, тро́гатель-
ный, and expressions like уби́ть вре́мя (translated word for word
from the French—*tuer le temps*), etc. We can find this kind of
language, capable of competing with French, in Karamzin's *Пи́сьма
ру́сского путеше́ственника*, in his stories, his critical studies and
publicist writings. These models exerted a tremendous influence on
the progressive section of the aristocracy. They penetrated into
private correspondence and later into speech, and in this way the
process already begun in the middle of the 18th century on the basis
of the 'middle style' developed further. To begin with the circle of
people who underwent this influence was not very big. The habit
of using French as the language for thoughts and feelings was so
deeply rooted that even a century later it still showed through in
certain circles. Not only did Pushkin's Tat′yana write her letter to
Onegin in French, since 'she had difficulty in expressing herself in
her mother tongue'—

> Выража́лася с трудо́м
> На языке́ своём родно́м,

but also the heroine of Boborykin's[1] story, *Без мужжéй* (c. 1880),
suffering from her inability to interest a possible fiancée, is described
in the following way:

Ей ста́ло доса́дно, что по-ру́сски она́ говори́т бесцве́тно: не хвата́ет слов.
Про́сто она́ глупе́ет. Будь э́то по-францу́зски, она́ бы ему́ в че́тверть ча́са
показа́ла, как она́ уме́ет говори́ть и ду́мать. На том языке́ гото́вые фра́зы.
Ими игра́ешь, как ша́риками. А тут на́до за́ново составля́ть фра́зы. И в
сало́нах их никогда́ не произно́сят.

It annoyed her that she spoke Russian colourlessly, there weren't enough
words. It made her seem stupid. If they had been talking in French, she would

---

[1] P. D. Boborykin (1836–1921), an extremely prolific writer in many genres.
[Ed.]

have shown him in a quarter of an hour how well she could speak and think. In that language there were ready-made phrases. You could play with them like balls. But now you had to think up new phrases. And they never used them in salons.

But the essential thing for the history of the Russian language is that nevertheless a group of people, albeit a small one, did exist, who could consider the language of *Пи́сьма ру́сского путеше́ственника* as entirely their own. Consider, for example, the following extract, from this work:

Отдохну́въ въ тракти́рѣ и напи́вшись ча́ю, пошёлъ я да́лѣе по бе́регу о́зера, чтобы ви́дѣть гла́вную сце́ну рома́на, селе́ніе Клара́нъ. Высо́кія густы́я дере́ва скрыва́ютъ его́ отъ нетерпѣли́выхъ взо́ровъ. Подошёлъ, и уви́дѣлъ — бѣдную ма́ленькую деревеньку, лежа́щую у подо́швы горъ, покры́тыхъ е́лями. Вмѣсто жили́ща Юлі́ина, столь прекра́сно опи́саннаго, предста́вился мнѣ ста́рый за́мокъ съ ба́шнями; суро́вая нару́жность его́ пока́зываетъ суро́вость тѣхъ времёнъ, въ кото́рыя онъ постро́енъ. Мно́гіе изъ та́мошнихъ жи́телей зна́ютъ Но́вую Элои́зу, и весьма́ дово́льны тѣмъ, что вели́кой Руссо́ просла́вилъ ихъ ро́дину, сдѣлавъ её сце́ной своего́ рома́на. Рабо́тающій поселя́нинъ, ви́дя тамъ любопы́тнаго прише́льца, говори́тъ ему́ съ усмѣ́шкою: ба́ринъ коне́чно чита́лъ Но́вую Элои́зу. Оди́нъ стари́къ пока́зывалъ мнѣ и тотъ лѣсо́къ, въ кото́ромъ, по Руссо́ву описа́нію, Юлія поцѣлова́ла въ пе́рвый разъ стра́стнаго Сен-Прё, и симъ маги́ческимъ прикоснове́ніемъ потресла́ въ нёмъ всю не́рвную систе́му его́. — За дереве́нькою во́лны о́зера омыва́ютъ стѣны укрѣплённого за́мка Шильйо́на; уны́лый шумъ ихъ склоня́етъ ду́шу къ меланхоли́ческой дремо́тѣ.

The question of how much in this language was carried over from the old book tradition and how much had always belonged to the everyday language (cf. on the one hand гла́вную, рабо́тающій, прикоснове́ніемъ, and on the other бе́регу, дереве́ньку etc.); how much in it was indigenous and how much came from the west—these questions already had in fact no practical importance and could interest only the traditionalists who continued to uphold the theory of the three styles. In the language which was gradually beginning to prevail at the beginning of the 19th century, the elements originating from various sources were no longer felt to belong to different styles, and had coalesced into a composite but unified whole.

An analogous process was going on in the poetic language of the new literature, in the language of Batyushkov, Zhukovsky and of their precursors and followers. As we have already pointed out in the preceding chapter, the bookish tradition was generally stronger in the language of poetry. As a result, even the so-called light poetry of the beginning of the 19th century abounds in slavonicisms which

were not carried into the general middle stock of Russian vocabulary
by the process of mixing of styles. But the slavonicisms in this poetry
had quite a different role—here they were being used not for the sake
of their lofty style (высота́), but to satisfy new stylistic demands for
which slavonicisms were as useful as words from other sources. In
this poetry Church Slavonic words like лани́ты 'cheeks' and пе́рси
'breast' had the same stylistic value as Russian words like камелёк
'hearth' or ручеёк 'stream', and words of foreign origin like ро́зы
or а́рфа. For example, Batyushkov:

> Ста́ну всю́ду развева́ть
> Лёгким уст прикоснове́ньем,
> Как зефи́ра дунове́ньем,
> От кашта́новых воло́с
> То́нкий за́пах све́жих роз.
> Если ли́лия листа́ми
> Ко груди́ твое́й прильнёт,
> Если я́ркими луча́ми
> В камельке́ ого́нь блеснёт,
> Если пла́мень потае́нный
> По лани́там пробежа́л,
> Если по́яс сокрове́нный
> Развяза́лся и упа́л, —
> Улыбни́ся, друг бесце́нный,
> Это я! — Когда́ же ты,
> Сном закры́в преле́стны о́чи,
> Обнажи́шь во мра́ке но́чи
> Роз и ли́лий красоты́,
> Я взлохну́...и глас мой то́мный,
> Арфы го́лосу подо́бный,
> Ти́хо в во́здухе умрёт.

Towards the end of this extract note how it makes no difference to
the poet whether he uses глас or го́лос. His choice is dictated by the
metre. The final result is the same as in prose—the origin of the word
in itself ceases to be the determining factor in its stylistic value.
Consider also Zhukovsky:

> И ста́рец зрит гостеприи́мной,
> Что гость его́ уны́л,
> И све́тлый огонёк он в ды́мной
> Печу́рке разложи́л.
> Плоды́ и зе́лень предлага́ет
> С припра́вой до́брых слов;
> Бесе́дой ску́ку озлаща́ет
> Медли́тельных часо́в.
> Кружи́тся ре́звый кот пред ни́ми;
> В углу́ кричи́т сверчо́к...

and further:

> Трепе́щут пе́рси, взор склоне́нный;
> Как ро́за, цвет лани́т...
> И де́ву-пре́лесть изумле́нный
> Отше́льник в го́сте зрит.

But side by side with light poetry at the beginning of the 19th century an important place in Russian literary life was occupied by a new kind of serious poetry. This tradition which produced the civic lyric poetry of Pushkin and the poetry of the Decembrists still needed slavonicisms as an essential rhetorical device, by means of which it not only attained the necessary 'elevation' of style but also its patriotic tone. Another device which was formerly little used, but at this time acquired a greater importance, was the use of archaisms of vocabulary and phraseology. These directly satisfied the need which had arisen to evoke olden times and lent greater expressiveness to the patriotic tone of the narrative. The use of such archaisms in Karamzin's *Исто́рия Госуда́рства Росси́йского* and in his historical stories was to have enormous significance for the Russian literary language in the first half of the nineteenth century. It is from this source that words and expressions like гри́вна 'medieval silver coin', ве́че 'veche' (assembly of citizens in old Rus'), о́троки 'boys, young retainers', дружи́на 'Prince's retinue', подру́чники 'vassals', бить чело́м 'to petition', опоя́сать мечо́м 'to buckle on a sword', and so on came to be used widely in literature. After using old Russian words and expressions Karamzin often adds comments on them, for example: 'ходи́ть в дань' зна́чило тогда́ 'объезжа́ть Росси́ю и собира́ть нало́ги', or 'стоя́ли всю ночь за щита́ми', т. е. 'вооружённые в боево́м поря́дке', etc. It is easy to see the reflection of this vocabulary and phraseology in such works as Ryleyev's *Ду́мы*, Kyukhelbeker's ballads and Zagoskin's novels.

The reformed literary language was an intensely vital thing, since it directly met the needs of literature and the environment which had created it. Apart from anything else its establishment as the ordinary written and spoken language of the educated layer of society was destined to make a significant contribution towards the abolition of the differences which existed between the literary and the everyday language in the sphere of morphology and pronunciation. Gradually vulgar forms like рубле́въ instead of рубле́й, въ пла́мѣ instead of пла́мени, etc., disappear from literary usage, but on the other hand

8-3

it becomes more difficult to use Slavonic forms like явльшійся instead of явйвшійся. By this time аканье ceases to be the sign of inferior speech; rhymes like розы—слёзы occur, which earlier were impossible, since the word слезы when stressed was pronounced with the vowel e; the pronunciation [ɣ] in place of г is gradually restricted to a few words like богáтый, блáго, бог.

It goes without saying however that the former literary language with all its variants did not immediately yield to the new. It was retained along with the new, as long as the kinds of literature requiring it remained current. For example even the innovators themselves, writers like Karamzin and Zhukovsky, continued to write odes and similar works. These odes were of course written in conformity with the rules of Classicism. And in general the old in the language did not yield to the new without a struggle. The struggle between the old and new styles, which flared up after the publication of Shishkov's *Рассуждéние о стáром и нóвом слóге российского языкá* in 1803, made a very big impact on the thinking minds of its day, and for many years to come its repercussions were still perceptible in Russian literature. But so far as the history of the Russian language was concerned this whole notable polemic was of almost no importance. It is interesting not from the point of view of linguistics, but on a much wider basis, that of *Weltanschauung*. Shishkov's ardent and sincere, but largely irresponsible, patriotism provided a prop for the convinced and conscious patriots of the younger literary generation, the future ideologists of the Decembrist Revolt (1825). They were afraid of the cosmopolitan look of the Karamzin school, which however did not in the least worry people like Pushkin. Where the question of language in itself was concerned, however, Shishkov, while clinging resolutely to the theory of the three styles, at the same time crudely distorted the essence of Lomonosov's doctrine, since he considered as high style not the heterogeneous Slavonic-Russian (славенороссийский) which contained an admixture of elements taken from the language of the ecclesiastical books, but purely and simply the language of the church itself. To the critics who pointed out that славéнский and рýсский were two different languages, Shishkov obstinately replied that they were not two different languages but two different styles of the same language—which perhaps would have made sense in the old Rus' of the days before Peter the Great—and he proposed to introduce Church Slavonic words like: лы́сто 'leg, shank', любопрѣніе 'argument', непщевáть 'consider', углѣбáть 'sink, founder', ýне 'better', усырéнный 'moist', etc. into literary usage. Of course no one ever wrote like this, not even Shishkov himself. It was all purely utopian and a far cry from the ideas of Lomonosov, whose name Shishkov revered. Shishkov's young disciples, like Kyukhelbeker, were also much closer to Karamzin in their language than they themselves imagined. Their polemic with the members of the Arzamas Society was the product of a discussion as to what poetry should be about and was expressed in the contrast of 'serious' poetry containing elevated civic themes, with the 'trifles' which flourished in the school of Karamzin and Dmitriev. (Compare Pushkin's witty objection in *Евгéний Онéгин*, chapter IV, xxxii–xxxiii.) But the same Kyukhelbeker subsequently acknowledged the value of Karamzin's style as a model to be emulated.

The practical significance of Shishkov's invective against the new style was partly that it forced writers at the beginning of the century to be somewhat more discriminating in their choice of words of western European origin. But even in this respect one should not exaggerate Shishkov's role. If we compare the text of the first edition of Karamzin's *Пи́сьма ру́сского путешéственника* (1791–2) with the second, we find that Karamzin eliminated an enormous number of borrowings. In 1797, six years before Shishkov's *Рассуждéнія*, in the second edition of Karamzin's *Пи́сьма* instead of о моёмъ воя́жѣ we find о моёмъ путешéствіи, instead of потóмъ публику́етъ о васъ we read потóмъ объяви́тъ о васъ, instead of натурáльно— как вóдится, instead of иску́сство въ баланси́рованіи—иску́сство въ пры́ганіи, etc. However, what Shishkov demanded was the complete renunciation of Europeanisms in Russian speech,[1] and he protested against the use even of such international words as морáльный, эстети́ческий, эпóха, сцéна, катастрóфа, герои́зм, энтузиáзм, гармóния, интерéс; and of phraseological gallicisms which had taken root in Russian usage, such as тóнкий вкус 'good taste', трóгать ду́шу 'to touch the heart', etc. On the whole we can

---

[1] Among the Church Slavonic neologisms recommended by Shishkov to replace foreign words were: instead of аудитóрия—слу́шалище, орáтор—краснослóв, биллиáрд—шарокáт, калóши—мокросту́пы, etc. Shishkov's passion for Slavonicisms was parodied by the members of the Arzamas society in the sentence: Хороши́лище идёт в мокросту́пах по гульби́щу из ристáлища на позóрище, i.e. Франт идёт в калóшах по бульвáру из ци́рка в теáтр. [Ed.]

say that the excesses indulged in by Russian writers at the end of the 18th and the beginning of the 19th centuries were recognised and rejected from the Russian literary language, independently of the opinions of Shishkov and his supporters.

But there was one really serious contradiction in the new style. It had been pointed out to some extent even by Shishkov, but he was unable to indicate any solution. The fact was that the polished, pure and elegant language which the literary innovators cultivated in books and society was devoid of genuine national character and lacked the flavour of everyday life and of real ' Russianness' (наро́дность). From a literary point of view this made it poor and inexpressive, and yet at the same time it remained too elegant for ordinary everyday affairs. The users of this purified noble language were afraid to bring into it a breath of vulgar speech (простонаро́дность) and triviality, and for this reason they avoided words which because of their meaning or stylistic colour, did not belong to the fashionable salon. In Karamzin's opinion words like квас or па́рень could not possibly be used in literature. Krylov was severely criticised because he did not keep the rule: изъясня́ться всегда́ пра́вильно и особли́во избега́ть слов, употребля́емых че́рнью 'always to express oneself correctly avoiding especially words used by the vulgar mob'; i.e. such colloquial words as: не моги́ the imperative of мочь, used only in the negative, стеречи for стере́чь, гуто́ря вздор 'blethering nonsense', гляди́-тко 'just look' (examples from A. Izmaylov). As a writer of fables Dmitriev was in general preferred to Krylov, precisely because his style was 'purer'. We can see the difference between their use of the language if we compare their respective versions of the same fable. Dmitriev begins his fable *Дуб и Трость* in this way:

Дуб с Тро́стию вступи́л одна́жды в разгово́ры.

And Krylov like this:

С трости́нкой Дуб одна́жды в речь вошёл.

Dmitriev:

Легча́йший ветеро́к, едва́ струя́щий во́ду.

Krylov:

Чуть лёгкий ветеро́к подёрнет ря́бью во́ду.

Dmitriev:

— Ты о́чень жа́лостлив, Трость Ду́бу отвеча́ла:
Но пра́во, о себе́ ещё я не вздыха́ла.

120

Krylov:

> — Ты о́чень жа́лостлив, сказа́ла Трость в отве́т,
> Одна́ко не круши́сь: мне сто́лько ху́да нет.

The language of Dmitriev's fable really is pure and simple, but it lacks the expressive 'Russianness' for which Krylov's fables are noted. Naturally the epigoni of Karamzinism continued to exaggerate this fear of 'vulgar speech', and it was they who were the creators of that tyrannical tradition of the speech of 'good society' and 'people with taste', which Pushkin found so irritating and which sometimes provided the occasion for very shrewd and amusing parodies, like the following passage taken from Narezhny's *Росси́йский Жиль-Бла́з*:

> Вме́сто того́, что́бы сказа́ть, как и бы́ло пре́жде: «Ма́тушка, мне пора́ накрыва́ть на стол? уже́ ба́тюшка пришёл с гумна́», она́ говори́ла: «Ma chère maman! Я име́ю ду́мать, что уже́ вре́мя ста́вить на стол куве́рты на пять персо́н; mon cher папа изво́лил возврати́ться из воя́жа, во вре́мя кото́рого изво́лил он осмотре́ть хозя́йственные заведе́ния каса́тельно хлебопа́шества.

This was how Katerina began to speak after she became engaged to one of the fashionable nobility. Thus if the Russian literary language really was to become a national one, it was necessary to break down the barrier which had arisen between the language used in the salon and in literature by the well-educated circle, and the language used by the man in the street. This was achieved in the twenties and thirties of the 19th century by writers of the post-Karamzin period, headed by Pushkin, whose name became to future generations the symbol of the unified Russian national language.

What is usually implied by Pushkin's role in the history of the language is that he was responsible for the new and final act of combining together the bookish and everyday elements of our language. For Pushkin the bookish element was embodied in the most outstanding and brilliant achievements of the Karamzin school, for example in Karamzin's *Исто́рия госуда́рства росси́йского*, and in the poetry of Batyushkov and Zhukovsky, while the everyday element was embodied in the works of Krylov or Fonvizin, that is, in the material of idiomatic popular speech on which are based the fables of Krylov, and which constitutes the speech of for instance the Prostakovs and Yeremeyevna in Fonvizin's *Не́доросль*. Pushkin's language in his mature works represents the unification of these two traditions, such a complete unification that the separate elements in it can no longer be labelled elegant or coarse in themselves, but are directly subordinated to the given context as a whole.

Therefore such vulgar and colloquial expressions as were current in the everyday household usage of those layers of cultured society which had preserved their links with the Russian people, find a place even in the most serious—'ва́жные' as they were then called—of Pushkin's works. For instance:

> Когда́ за го́родом, заду́мчив я брожу́
> И на публи́чное кладби́ще захожу́,
> Решётки, сто́лбики, наря́дные гробни́цы,
> Под ко́ими гнию́т все мертвецы́ столи́цы,
> В боло́те кое-как стеснённые рядко́м,
> Как го́сти жа́дные за ни́щенским столо́м,
> Купцо́в, чино́вников усо́пших мавзоле́и,
> Дешёвого резца́ неле́пые зате́и,
> Над ни́ми на́дписи и в про́зе и в стиха́х
> О доброде́телях, о слу́жбе и чина́х;
> По ста́ром рогаче́ вдови́цы плач аму́рный
> Вора́ми со столбо́в отви́нченные у́рны,
> Моги́лы скли́зкие, кото́ры та́кже тут
> Зева́ючи жильцо́в к себе́ на у́тро ждут —
> Таки́е сму́тные мне мы́сли всё наво́дит,
> Что зло́е на меня́ уны́ние нахо́дит.
> Хоть плю́нуть, да бежа́ть...

Or in another poem *Доро́жные жа́лобы*:

> До́лго ль мне в тоске́ голо́дной
> Пост нево́льный соблюда́ть.
> И теля́тиной холо́дной
> Трю́фли Яра помина́ть.

Or in *Ме́дный вса́дник*:

> Вода́ сбыла́, и мостова́я
> Откры́лась, и Евге́ний мой
> Спеши́т, душо́ю замира́я,
> В наде́жде, стра́хе и тоске́
> К едва́ смири́вшейся реке́.
> Но, торжество́м побе́ды по́лны,
> Ещё кипе́ли зло́бно во́лны,
> Как бы под ни́ми тлел ого́нь,
> Ещё их пе́на покрыва́ла,
> И тяжело́ Нева́ дыша́ла,
> Как с би́твы прибежа́вший конь.
> Евге́ний смо́трит: ви́дит ло́дку,
> Он к ней бежи́т, как на нахо́дку,
> Он перево́зчика зовёт —

> И перево́зчик беззабо́тный
> Его́ за гри́венник охо́тно
> Чрез во́лны стра́шные везёт.

Everyone can recall 'vulgar' words and mundane everyday expressions which occur even in Pushkin's most intimate lyrical poems, in his Byronic narrative poems, in the most accomplished of his works, such as the little tragedies, the narrative poem *Тази́т*, etc. For example, we read in his poem *Осень*—

> Тепе́рь моя́ пора́: я не люблю́ весны́,
> Скучна́ мне о́ттепель, вонь, грязь — весно́й я бо́лен…

and further:

> Дни по́здней о́сени браня́т обыкнове́нно,
> Но мне она́ мила́, чита́тель дорого́й,
> Красо́ю ти́хою, блиста́ющей смире́нно.
> Так нелюби́мое дитя́ в семье́ родно́й
> К себе́ меня́ влечёт. Сказа́ть вам открове́нно,
> Из годовы́х времён я рад лишь ей одно́й…

Compare *Тазит*:

> Поди́ ты прочь — ты мне не сын.
> Ты не чече́нец — ты стару́ха,
> Ты трус, ты раб, ты армяни́н.
> Будь про́клят мной. Поди́ — чтоб слу́ха
> Никто́ о ро́бком не име́л,
> Чтоб ве́чно ждал ты гро́зной встре́чи,
> Чтоб мёртвый брат тебе́ на пле́чи
> Окровавлённой ко́шкой сел
> И к бе́здне гнал тебя́ неща́дно,
> Чтоб ты, как ра́неный оле́нь,
> Бежа́л, тоскуя́ безотра́дно,
> Чтоб де́ти ру́сских дереве́нь
> Тебя́ верёвкою пойма́ли
> И как волчо́нка затерза́ли,
> Чтоб ты…беги́…беги́ скоре́й,
> Не оскверня́й мои́х оче́й!

There is no need even to mention such works as *Бори́с Годуно́в* and *Капита́нская до́чка*, in which Pushkin reproduces the actual speech of simple people.

Pushkin repeatedly pointed out to the defenders of good taste and of the polished refined language how chimerical and false their ideal was. Pushkin's friend Vyazemsky once said very shrewdly that only a lackey would feel awkward about pronouncing a word like воня́ет 'stinks' in society, and that a cultivated person would say this word boldly even in a high-society drawing room and in front of ladies. It

Creation of the national standard language

was exactly in this spirit that Pushkin wrote in one of the subsequently
discarded stanzas for *Евгéний Онéгин*:

> В гостúной свéтской и свобóдной
> Был прúнят слог простонарóдный
> И не пугáл ничьúх ушéй
> Живóю стрáнностью своéй.

In literary disputes too, Pushkin resolutely opposed the convention-
ality of fashionable proprieties and in this context also supported his
opinion by referring to the customary usage of the language 'В
óбществе вы лóктем задéли сосéда вáшего, вы извинáетесь —
óчень хорошó. — Но гулáя в толпé под качéлями, толкнýли
лáвочника — вы не скáжете емý: mille pardons. Вы зовёте
извозчика — и говорúте емý: *пошёл в Колóмну*, а не — *сдéлайте
одолжéние, потрудúтесь свезтú в Колóмну.*' Pushkin's firm conviction that it was unnecessary and impossible to fix hard and fast
limits between the living language of everyday life and the standard
literary language shows distinctly in all his polemical and critical
writings.

It has already been noted that Pushkin found support for this
conviction in Krylov's fables, in Fonvizin's comedies and in other
literary works remarkable for the 'Russianness' of their language.
But Pushkin would never have been able to bring about a successful
realization of his idea of the Russian literary language had he
known Russian popular speech only from literary examples. He
drew strength for his feat straight from the source of the language of
the people—from their folk poetry, from their ways of thought, from
the world of national traditions and customs, from the past of the
Russian people and the Russian state. His eager interest in everything
in contemporary Russia that bore the stamp of national culture
(нарóдность) is well known. Suffice it here to point out that if
Pushkin had not had such a close bond with the Russian people,
with its mode of life, with its history and psychology, then the great
synthesis of the literary and folk elements in the Russian language
created by the writings of Pushkin and his contemporaries would
never have been achieved. We must add here that in Pushkin's time
and above all in Pushkin's own works there is a marked decrease in
the use of poetic diction: in particular the pronunciation used in
verse becomes closer to that of ordinary speech. Shishkov still
continued to demand that in elevated style the word горá should be

pronounced with an *o* and the sound [ɣ] instead of г, but this was already, in the full sense of the word, a thing of the past by the second and third decades of the 19th century. Generally speaking Pushkin was not so much the reformer as the great liberator of Russian speech from the multitudinous trammels of convention. Simplicity, naturalness, a feeling of moderation and complete internal freedom in the selection of means of expression are the characteristics of Pushkin's language, from the point of view both of vocabulary and also of compositional structure. Karamzin's elegantly finished but frequently ornate and long-winded syntax was superseded under the pen of Pushkin by an energetic, precise laconicism and a compressed business-like tone of exposition. Here are two extracts for comparison from Karamzin's *Рыцарь нашего времени* and Pushkin's *Дубровский*. Firstly, Karamzin:

На луговой стороне Во́лги, там, где впада́ет в неё прозра́чная река́ Свия́га, и где, как изве́стно по Исто́рии Ната́льи, Боя́рской до́чери, жил и у́мер изгна́нником неви́нный Боя́рин Любосла́вский — там, в ма́ленькой дереве́ньке, роди́лся пра́дед, дед, отец Лео́нов; там роди́лся и сам Лео́н, в то вре́мя, когда́ Приро́да, подо́бно любе́зной коке́тке, сидя́щей за туале́том, убира́лась, наряжа́лась в лу́чшее своё весе́ннее пла́тье; бели́лась, румя́нилась...весе́нними цвета́ми; смотре́лась с улы́бкою в зе́ркало...вод прозра́чных, и завива́ла себе́ ку́дри...на верши́нах древе́сных — то есть...

Secondly, Pushkin:

По́хороны соверши́лись на тре́тий день. Те́ло бе́дного старика́ лежа́ло на столе́, покры́тое са́ваном и окружённое свеча́ми. Столо́вая полна́ была́ дворо́вых. Гото́вились к вы́носу. Влади́мир и тро́е слуг по́дняли гроб. Свяще́нник пошёл вперёд, дьячо́к сопровожда́л его́, воспева́я погреба́льные моли́твы. Хозя́ин Кистеневки в после́дний раз перешёл за поро́г своего́ до́ма. Гроб понесли́ ро́щею. Це́рковь находи́лась за не́ю. День был я́сный и холо́дный. Осе́нние ли́стья па́дали с дере́в.

A closer study of this style belongs to the history of Russian literature and not to the history of the Russian language. But the link is obvious between the astonishing and mature simplicity of construction of Pushkin's language, between his striving for 'пре́лесть наго́й простоты́' and his hostility towards artificial partitions separating literary usage from the living language. Thus it was in Pushkin that the national language achieved the standard towards which all the complex developments taking place in the language from the end of the 17th century had tended.

11

THE LITERARY LANGUAGE
IN THE 19TH AND 20TH CENTURIES

It follows from what has been said that it was the language of Russian literature which was called upon to play the decisive role in the final stages of the movement towards a national standard language. This was because it was in Pushkin's time that Russian literature set itself tasks in which it was hindered by the artificial division between the language of 'good society' and that of everyday life. It is fairly obvious that this was a movement towards that artistic realism which became so evident about the middle of Pushkin's literary career. At this crucial time in the development of the national language the requirements of the literary language and those of the language used for non-literary purposes were extremely similar. Once the national standard had appeared, however, the needs of literature and of other types of writing once again diverged, with consequent effects upon the further history of the language.

As we saw in the previous chapter, the written language which prevailed at the beginning of the 19th century was too involved and elegant for general purposes, and at the same time somewhat insipid and anaemic so far as the requirements of literature were concerned. But the age of Pushkin, by raising the banner of 'nationality' (наро́дность) in language, discovered the true basis for an expressive literary language. Consequently it liberated the Russian language at this point in its development from the pursuit of specifically aesthetic aims, and left it to find its functions as a national standard language. It became clear, on the one hand, that the national standard language did not have to be a specifically literary language, but on the other hand that the literary language did not have to restrict itself to those resources which the standard language provided. This is why the history of Russian during the 19th and 20th centuries consists to a considerable extent of the separate histories of the national standard language and of the language of Russian literature.

The 19th and 20th centuries

Let us begin with the latter. Since the basic material of the great Russian realist literature of the 19th and 20th centuries was provided by the authentic realities of Russian life, realist writers could not but include among their tasks the reproduction of living Russian speech in its multifarious forms reflecting occupational, social and dialect differences. Especially after the remarkable achievements of the school of Gogol', the use, for purposes of characterisation, of details and nuances from the speech of various groups in society became one of the constant preoccupations of Russian writers. Another factor which dictated this interest in the living language at its most direct was the high level of achievement attained in the field of psychological analysis, culminating in the works of Tolstoy, Dostoyevsky, and their successors. All this explains why, from the time of Gogol' onwards, a great flood of varied non-literary linguistic material poured into Russian literature, drawn from such sources as peasant dialects, the speech of tradesmen and merchants, and also from the peculiar mental states of heroes with either rich or impoverished spiritual lives. All this varied material provided the realists with one of their most important means of creating literary types, with the raw material for the moulding of images and above all for the construction of dialogue.

Thus an enormous field of linguistic material had opened up before the writer. Not only features of pronunciation, but grammatical and especially lexical and phraseological features were blended with literary usage. Peasant speech was of particular importance, and one of the most remarkable masters in this field was Tolstoy. The speech of peasants in Tolstoy's works reproduces exactly the language of the village—in so far as this is possible and permissible in a printed work—but at the same time he uses peasant speech with discrimination, so that his works do not become a mere ethnographic museum. The play *Власть тьмы* is of particular interest in this respect. In it phonetic peculiarities are almost completely ignored, but the vocabulary and syntax are faithfully reproduced, e.g.

Матрёна. Ну, но́вости сказа́ла! А тётка Матрёна и не зна́ла. Эх, де́ушка, тётка Матрёна тёрта, тёрта да перетёрта. Тётка Матрёна, я тебе́ скажу́, я́годка! под землёй-то на арши́н ви́дит. Всё зна́ю, я́годка! Зна́ю, заче́м молоды́м ба́бам со́нных порошко́в на́доть. Принесла́... Чего надо́-то ви́жу, а чего́ не на́до, того́ знать не зна́ю, ве́дать не ве́даю. Так-то. То́же и тётка Матрёна молода́я была́. То́же с свои́м дурако́м, ве́дашь, уме́ючи прожи́ть на́до. Все 77 увёрток зна́ю. Ви́жу, я́годка, зачивря́л, зачивря́л твой-то стари́к. С чем тут жить? Его́ ви́лами ткни, кровь не пойдёт. Гля́дишь, на

127

весну́ похоро́нишь. Приня́ть во двор кого́-нибудь да на́до. А сыно́к чем не мужи́к. Не ху́же люде́й. Так что же мне за коры́сть сы́на-то с до́брого де́ла снять? Ра́зве я своему́ дети́щу враг?

In other cases Tolstoy also renders the pronunciation of his characters. For instance, in *Севасто́польские расска́зы* one of the soldiers says у се́рдце гхори́ть 'my heart is burning'. This shows the South Russian у instead of в before an initial consonant, and the velar fricative [ɣ] instead of the literary г, as well as the soft т in the ending of the third person singular. In the same place we find ны́нче так бьёть, что бяда́ 'now [the enemy] is really giving us it hot' (тепе́рь так бьёт, что беда́); вот она́ аж че́рез несёть 'that one [bomb] is going right over us'; большу́щая така́я ядро́ 'such an enormous cannon-ball'. In *Власть тьмы* we find: слыха́мши (слыха́вши), куфа́рка (куха́рка), пра́вов нет (прав нет), сило́м (наси́льно), new vocative forms such as Мики́т (from Мики́та), Аку́ль (from Аку́ля),[1] etc. In general, leaving aside the question of the relative skill or discretion of individual writers, this is the process which familiarised the reader of Russian in the 19th and 20th centuries with such phenomena of pronunciation, grammar and vocabulary as: ён (он), ма́ненько (немно́го), тепе́ря (тепе́рь), вчера́сь (вчера́), завсегда́ (всегда́), ба́ить (говори́ть), гута́рить (говори́ть), ляда́щий (плохо́й—'как говоря́т у нас в Орле́' is Turgenev's explanation of this word), нешто́ (неуже́ли), о́ченно (о́чень), боле́зный (серде́чный), должно́ (должно́ быть) and many others. There were of course cases of misuse, where certain authors became swamped in their ethnographic material and lost their sense of proportion. It was such cases which led to protests like that contained in a well known letter from Chekhov to his brother in 1889: 'Beware of *recherché* language. Language should be simple and elegant. Servants should speak simply, without all sorts of "пуща́й" and "тапе́рича".' It should, however, be said that the works of writers who knew the Russian village well and had a feeling for language contain a fund of dialectological material which linguists have not yet exploited as they ought.

An important problem in the history of the language of Russian literature in the 19th and 20th centuries is the speech of characters of a semi-literate type, that is, people who have come into contact with

---

[1] These are truncated forms of personal names ending in -a or -я, cf. also мам 'Mummy', пап 'Daddy'. [Ed.]

The 19th and 20th centuries

urban civilisation in a purely superficial way but whose spiritual development remains at a primitive level. They represent a peculiar, rotten product of capitalist civilisation which gave birth to outcasts who, while they have lost touch with the mass of the people, have not found a place among the ranks of the cultured class. This is the world of the Russian petty-bourgeois (мещáнство) and merchantry which we find so vividly portrayed in the works of Gogol', Ostrovsky, Dostoyevsky, Saltykov-Shchedrin, [Leskov], Chekhov and Gor'ky. The literature of the late 19th and early 20th centuries reproduces with remarkable skill the ugly, distorted speech of this world in which the pure, vivid speech of the people is replaced by ill-digested, meaningless snatches of the sophisticated language of the intelligentsia. Yepikhodov in Chekhov's *Вишнёвый сад* is a noteworthy figure of this type. This is how he speaks:

Но, конéчно, éсли взглянýть с тóчки зрéния, то вы, позвóлю себé так вы́разиться, извини́те за откровéнность, совершéнно привели́ меня́ в состоя́ние дýха.

Such speech is characterised by an abundance of interjections and by fragmented phrases: с тóчки зрéния—we do not know which point of view; в состоя́нии дýха—what state?, and so on. The origin of such language is explained with complete accuracy by Yepikhodov himself:

Я развитóй человéк, читáю рáзные замечáтельные кни́ги, но никáк не могý поня́ть направлéния, чегó мне сóбственно хóчется, жить мне, и́ли застрели́ться, сóбственно говоря́, но тем не мéнее я всегдá ношý при себé револьвéр.

The speech of people who, like the telegraphist Yat' in Chekhov's *Свáдьба*, 'хóчут сво́ю образóванность показáть', appears in many forms and cannot be reduced to a single formula. Here belong the intoxicated overbearing merchant shouting in the club: прошý мне не претикослóвить [a conflation of прекослóвить 'contradict' and преткновéние 'stumbling']; the peasant's son living in town who sends his parents a pound of tea: для удовлетворéния их физи́ческой потрéбности 'for the satisfaction of their physical requirements'; the warehouseman (прикáзчик) whose worldly wisdom takes the form of such phrases as соотвéтствие жи́зни по амби́ции ли́чности—literally 'correspondence of one's life with the pride of the personality'—or всё зави́симо от волнéния креди́та 'everything is dependent upon the fluctuation of credit', and who

129

orders some tongue in a restaurant with the words: Дай-ка нам порцию главного мастера клеветы и злословия с картофельным пюре 'Give us a portion of the great expert in slander and gossip with creamed potatoes'; and many others. This material in our literature is of great importance for the study of the processes of concentration and stratification which took place in the language of the Russian people as capitalism developed.

Of particular interest are the 'linguistic masks' which Russian writers give to their characters in order to create individualised psychological portraits or to depict particular mental states. For instance, Gogol′ sometimes uses a kind of language consisting mainly of interjections and pronouns, which has no real content but merely suggests certain confused mental processes. An outstanding example of this is the expletive того constantly used by Akakiy Akakievich in *Шинель.* Compare, for example:

Да, конечно, нельзя сказать, чтоб не было того в своём роде...Ну, конечно, кто ж против этого и стоит, чтобы опять не было...Где ж, так сказать, а впрочем...да, да.

Or again:

Признаюсь, это уж совсем непостижимо, это точно...нет! нет! Совсем не понимаю...А однако же при всём том, хотя, конечно, можно допустить и то и другое и третье, может даже...ну, да и где не бывает несообразностей...а всё однако ж...есть что-то.

This style of speech was frequently imitated by other writers, for instance, by Turgenev in *Петушков.* Another phenomenon of this kind is the incorporation of linguistic features in character portraits, so that a character is described not only in terms of his appearance and dress, but also of his manner of speech. The younger Verkhovensky in Dostoyevsky's *Бесы* is a good example:

His enunciation is extraordinarily clear, so that his words pour out like large, equally sized beads, always well-chosen and always ready to be turned on. At first you find this pleasing, but it soon palls, precisely because of this excessively clear enunciation and these ever-ready strings of words. And you get the feeling that his tongue must be of a special shape, unusually long and thin, terribly red and with an extremely pointed tip which is constantly wagging without its owner's volition.

Kirillov's speech is different:

He seemed somewhat contemplative and absent-minded. He spoke jerkily and somehow ungrammatically, arranging the words in a strange order and getting mixed up if he had to compose a sentence of any length.

The 19th and 20th centuries

Here is an example of Kirillov's speech:

Старýшка свекрóвь приéхала; нет, снохá...всё равнó. Три дня. Лежи́т больнáя, с ребёнком, по ночáм кричи́т óчень, живóт. Мать спит, а старýха принóсит; я мячóм. Мяч из Гáмбурга. Я в Гáмбурге купи́л, чтóбы бросáть и лови́ть: укрепля́ет спи́ну. Дéвочка.

The conditions for the development of the language of poetry were different. It participated only to a limited degree in the movement towards individualised characterisation, and in the case of lyrical poetry—the most important side of Russian poetry—such considera-ions were practically irrelevant. Therefore the language of poetry at the end of the 19th century was much nearer that of the beginning of the century than was the case with prose. In the 20th century certain changes have taken place in the language of poetry, chiefly in con-nection with Futurism and the poetry of Mayakovsky, but this question is beyond the scope of the present work.

Here we can deal with only a few of the large number of problems connected with the history of the Russian literary language. Obviously there is an overlap here between linguistic and literary problems. But alongside the history of the use of Russian for literary purposes—whether it be the standard national language or various local, social or individual variants—there continued the history of the national standard language as the instrument of Russian culture and politics. The general lines of development during the 19th and 20th centuries are as follows.

This was the period in which the phonetic and grammatical norms of Russian became established, and in which great strides were made towards universal standards of orthography. We saw in chapter 10 that at the beginning of the 19th century the language of the cultured class still contained various elements inconsistent with the norms of the written language. These included: the Russianised pronunciation of some loan-words, e.g. анбáр instead of амбáр, шаппáнское instead of шампáнское, in which dissimilation took place between the nasal and non-nasal labials; the pronunciation of ры instead of ри between consonants, e.g. скры́пка, грыбы́; the pronunciation of ч as ш before н in a much larger number of cases than at the present day, e.g. свешнóй instead of свечнóй; such forms as ребя́ты (ребя́та), кóльцы (кóльца), к тéмю (к тéмени), три дни (три дня), к емý (к немý), к стáте (к стáти), etc. During the 19th century these hangovers of 'common speech' (простонарóдность) died out among

131

educated speakers of Russian under the influence of schools and of such grammarians as Grech, Vostokov and others, whose works reflected the already established norms of standard literate speech. At the same time the process of standardising the orthography went ahead. In the first decades of the 19th century many of the most cultured people used spelling which by modern standards would be considered illiterate. Griboyedov wrote лезить (instead of лѣзетъ), кормановъ (карма́новъ), давиче (да́веча), на еву (на яву́), старичь-ковъ (старичко́въ); Pushkin wrote каляска (коля́ска), окуратный (аккура́тный), голинькой (го́ленький), прозьба (про́сьба), завяски (завя́зки), etc. Karamzin had reason to complain that 'it is extremely difficult to find a teacher of the Russian language, and I doubt whether one could find in the whole country a hundred people who have a thorough knowledge of the orthography'. Things were different by the end of the century as a result of the considerable growth in the importance of schools. Of course many controversial and obscure problems of orthography remained—even today, after the reforms of 1917, there are quite a number—and decisions on such problems had to be made somehow in pedagogical circles. The most important attempt to regularise the orthography was that of academician Ya. Grot (1886). And although the mass of the population remained illiterate, and Grot's orthography was none too easy for a person of average culture, at least the most highly educated people at the end of the 19th century could spell fairly well 'по Гро́ту'. Further successes in the field of literacy belong to the post-revolutionary epoch. Two measures carried out by the new régime—the reform of the orthography (i.e. the abolition of unnecessary archaic letters, and spellings) and the introduction of universal primary education—really made literacy a national concern.

At the same time the vocabulary of the national language continued to expand. The development of social and philosophical ideas, along with new discoveries in history and the natural sciences, created a demand for new words, or for the adaptation of old ones to denote new concepts in intellectual life and science. We shall mention the three basic processes which provided this enrichment of vocabulary. Firstly, word-formation based on patterns characteristic of the learned language, including many words with the suffixes -ние and -тель, such as рукоплеска́ние, голосова́ние, де́ятель, вдохнови́тель, and words like нау́чный, дарови́тый, тво́рчество, действи́тель-

132

ность, влия́тельный, etc. Secondly, there appeared a considerable number of *calques* or loan-translations based on foreign models. In the middle of the century, at the time when German idealistic philosophy was popular, use was made of various German models (which in their turn were frequently derived from Latin or Greek). Examples are прекраснодушие 'Schönseligkeit', and мировоз-зре́ние 'Weltanschauung'. Other words were given new meanings on the analogy of foreign models: for example, призва́ние, used by Pushkin in its original meaning of 'invitation' (приди́ на дру́жное призва́нье) comes to mean 'vocation' (чу́вствовать призва́ние к нау́ке); or односторо́нний 'one-sided' in the figurative meaning 'limited, narrow-minded'. Thirdly, the language continued to absorb at a great rate international terminology in the field not only of the natural sciences, but also of social and political ideas. Such terms were derived from the Classical languages, primarily Latin, e.g. факт, результа́т, прогре́сс, соли́дный, солида́рный, формули́ро-вать, воти́ровать, резюми́ровать, etc. Similarly, new suffixes derived from foreign sources began to appear in Russian, e.g. -изм: аскети́зм, мистици́зм, обскуранти́зм, and -изация: поляриза́ция, паупериза́ция, etc. This led to such words as цари́зм and the modern воениза́ция [in which Russian roots are combined with non-Russian suffixes. Ed.].

Needless to say, in the initial stages of this process, just as at the beginning of the 19th century, we come across abuse and a craze for the use of neologisms, particularly among second-rate writers and imitators. We get some idea of this fashion from the many jibes and parodies which appear in the literature of mid-century. For instance, in *Мёртвые ду́ши* Chichikov comes across a six-volume work in the library of Colonel Koshkaryov bearing the title *Предуготови́тель-ное вступле́ние к тео́рии мышле́ния. Тео́рия о́бщности, совоку́п-ности, су́щности, и в примене́нии к уразуме́нию органи́ческих нача́л обще́ственной производи́тельности.* We read further: 'Wherever Chichikov opened the book, on every page there was проявле́нье, разви́тье, абстра́кт, за́мкнутость and со́мкнутость, and the devil knows what else.'

Compare also this passage in one of Nekrasov's stories: 'All they can talk about is Hegel and Schlegel. They start to discuss Griboyedov and go off on to the creation of the world. Honestly, all their "individualities", their "unities", their "normalities" and "abstractions" (в их индивидуа́льностях, едини́чностях, в их норма́ль-ностях и абстра́ктностях) amount to nothing but nonsense—"grandiose" (as they say) nonsense.'

This brings to mind Herzen's account in *Было́е и ду́мы* of the days of 'rampant Hegelianism' (отча́янный гегели́зм) when 'close friends parted company for weeks on end because they had disagreed over the definition of "перехва́тывающий дух" or took as a personal insult some opinion concerning "абсолю́тная ли́чность" and its existence in itself.' We read further:

These young philosophers accepted...a kind of conventional language. They did not translate into Russian, but construed word for word, and to make things still easier they left all the Latin words *in crudo*, simply giving them Orthodox endings and the seven Russian cases. I have the right to say this, because I myself was carried along by that flood and wrote in exactly the same manner, and was even astonished that the famous astronomer Perevoshchikov referred to this as gobbledygook (пти́чий язы́к). At that time no one would have balked at such a sentence as: Конкресци́рование абстра́ктных иде́й в сфе́ре пла́стики пред-ставля́ет ту фа́зу самои́щущего ду́ха, в кото́рой он, определя́ясь для себя́, потенци́руется из есте́ственной имманс́нтности в гармони́ческую сфе́ру о́бразного созна́ния в красоте́. It is remarkable that here, as at that well-known dinner-party of generals which Yermolov spoke about, the Russian words sound more foreign than the Latin.

But the same Herzen in his mature years gives us a model of what journalistic writing should be: precise and clear, despite the fact that it has absorbed all that is essential and useful from the most up-to-date terminology and phraseology:

Нельзя́ не разделя́ть здоро́вый, реалисти́ческий взгляд, кото́рый в после́днее вре́мя, в одно́м из лу́чших ру́сских обозре́ний, стал выбива́ть то́щую мора́льную то́чку зре́ния на францу́зский мане́р, и́щущую ли́чной отве́т-ственности в о́бщих явле́ниях. Истори́ческие слои́ так же ху́до, как геологи́-ческие, обсу́живаются уголо́вной пала́той. И лю́ди, говоря́щие, что не на взя́точников и казнокра́дов сле́дует обру́шивать гро́мы и стре́лы, а на сре́ду, де́лающую взя́тки зоологи́ческим при́знаком це́лого пле́мени, наприме́р, *безборо́дых ру́сских*, соверше́нно правы́. Мы то́лько и жела́ем, чтоб никола́евские ли́шние лю́ди состоя́ли на права́х взя́точников и по́льзо-вались бы привиле́гиями, даро́ванными казнокра́дами. Они́ э́то тем бо́льше заслужи́ли, что они́ не то́лько ли́шние лю́ди, но почти́ все — лю́ди уме́ршие, а взя́точники и казнокра́ды живу́т, и не то́лько в дово́льстве, но и в истори́-ческом оправда́нии. С кем тут сража́ться, над кем смея́ться? С одно́й стороны́, упа́вшие от утомле́ния, с друго́й — помя́тые маши́ной; вини́ть их за э́то так же невеликоду́шно, как вини́ть золоту́шных и лимфати́ческих дете́й за худосо́чие их роди́телей.

In this passage, in contrast with the preceding example, it is quite clear that the Latin words sound entirely Russian. The same is true of language used for strictly scientific exposition, as for example in the following extract from Pisarev:

Для дре́вних о́бществ, постро́енных на ра́бстве, э́та возмо́жность не существова́ла. В э́тих о́бществах свобо́дный граждани́н, обеспе́ченный в своём существова́нии, мог, не роня́я своего́ досто́инства, занима́ться то́лько и́ли поли́тикой, и́ли филосо́фией, и́ли свобо́дными худо́жествами. Когда́ водворя́лся вое́нный деспоти́зм, тогда́ поли́тика отнима́лась прочь. Остава́лись филосо́фия и худо́жества. Но филосо́фия име́ла како́й-нибудь смысл то́лько тогда́, когда́ она́ гото́вила челове́ка для де́ятельной и общеполе́зной жи́зни, то есть всё-таки для полити́ческой карье́ры. Когда́ филосо́фия лиша́лась э́той еди́нственной це́ли, она́ жи́во превраща́лась в бессмы́сленное фразёрство и́ли в боле́зненную мечта́тельность. Вме́сто мы́слящих гра́ждан, она́ начина́ла формирова́ть ри́торов и́ли ми́стиков. Что же каса́ется до худо́жеств, то они́, по свое́й изве́стной ги́бкости, применя́лись ко всему́ и, находя́сь в деморализо́ванном о́бществе, станови́лись неме́дленно ре́вностными пропаганди́стами ни́зости и неле́пости. Так как при ра́бском труде́ прикладны́е нау́ки не могли́ ни возни́кнуть, ни развива́ться, то поня́тно, что в о́бществе, подчини́вшемся вое́нному деспоти́зму, должны́ бы́ли с изуми́тельной быстрото́й атрофи́роваться и́ли искажа́ться у́мственные спосо́бности, лишённые вся́кого пра́вильного и здоро́вого упражне́ния.

In these last two examples dating from the middle of the 19th century there is already almost nothing that could not be expressed in exactly the same words today. Both in grammar and vocabulary these texts are such that only a specialist in the subject could suspect that they belong to a time separated from ours by seven or eight decades. This is not to say, of course, that Russian has remained entirely unchanged since that time. On the contrary, we know that in these seventy to eighty years it has not only continued to evolve along the previous lines of development, but has felt the effects of the momentous events of the First World War and the October Revolution. This period has brought new words such as комсомо́л 'Young Communist League', колхо́з 'collective farm'; new meanings for existing words such as бригади́р 'brigadier', уда́рник 'shock-worker'; new spheres of usage for existing words such as комисса́р 'commissar'; new phenomena in word-formation such as аги́тка 'propagandist work of art', изба́ч 'keeper of a village reading-room'; a vast number of complex contractions used chiefly to describe new phenomena in the post-war and post-revolutionary periods [such as Совнарко́м < Сове́т Наро́дных Комисса́ров 'Council of People's Commissars', МТС < маши́нно-тра́кторная ста́нция 'machine and tractor station'], etc. But at the same time—and this is an extremely important feature in the life of the Russian language in this period—the common written language formed in the second half of the 19th century has become part and parcel of contemporary Soviet culture, making the Russian language of the Soviet period a 'traditional' language in the best and most precise sense of the word.

This tradition has been threatened to some extent by the encroachment of elements from the vulgar speech of particular social groups and from dialects, but the language of the Soviet period has coped with this problem, thanks largely to the irreproachable precision and foresight of Soviet government policy. The campaign for a high level of general literacy, for the purity and precision of language as one of the most important conditions for cultural progress, has been a constant feature of a great variety of measures brought in by the Soviet government and the Bolshevik Party...

One of Lenin's biographers has this to say:

> When Vladimir Il'ich was preparing any writings, decrees or declarations to be addressed to the masses, he himself always bore in mind, and demanded of others that they should bear in mind, that everything intended for the masses must be examined with extreme care, must be expressed in language of particular simplicity but without the slightest vulgarity...He could not tolerate...the style that had become accepted in newspapers, and which was frequently so insipid, difficult, boring and incomprehensible, that Vladimir Il'ich would exclaim while reading a paper: 'What language is this written in? Some kind of gibberish? This is Volapük, and not the language of Tolstoy and Turgenev!'

Lenin was particularly scathing about people who showed off by using learned words and who cluttered up Russian with totally unnecessary foreign borrowings. In his memorandum *On the Purification of the Russian Language* (Об очи́стке ру́сского языка́) Lenin declares total war on the pretence of scholarship and culture which seizes upon fashionable words as a means of hiding its own spiritual nakedness...

Lenin's mockery of his contemporaries' learned pretensions in language is well known. Bukharin's use of the word лимити́руются instead of ограни́чиваются occasioned the comical rejoinder: 'О, академи́зм! О, ложноклассици́зм! О, Тредьяко́вский!'...Yet Lenin objected strongly to any attempt to use specially simplified language for communication with the masses, considering this to be insulting to them...In his own writings Lenin always strove to raise the reader to his level, to make him literate in the national standard language of literature and learning, taking him beyond the vernacular. It was Lenin's practice, for instance, to gloss terms of foreign origin which he used, e.g. в дела́х купцо́в и фабрика́нтов наступи́ла зами́нка, так называ́емый кри́зис, оr организа́ция (то есть объедине́ние, сою́з) мирско́го крестья́нства колосса́льна (то есть огро́мна, необъя́тна), оr нивелиро́вка (выра́внивание) усло́вий жи́зни в больши́х города́х всего́ ми́ра, etc.

It is this middle-of-the-road policy on the written language, on the one hand keeping it at a high level of contemporary culture and on the other not permitting it to be divorced from its native roots, which is the main line of the Soviet government's linguistic policy...

In literature Gor'ky was the embodiment of this line of development. After going through a critical period at the beginning of the 20th century, it seems that contemporary Russian literature now favours a style of language in which the author, quite apart from the problem of conveying the speech of his characters in a convincing and individualised way, in his own narrative at least eschews the imitation of the peculiarities of language proper to his characters, and adheres to the norms of the standard language. Gor'ky consistently preached the need to follow these norms, guarding equally against an excessively bookish or ornate style and against the over-use in literature of vulgarisms and provincialisms. He wrote:

Why does he have to write вече́рняя сери́на́ [instead of су́мерки] оr скукожи́лся [instead of съёжился, сморщи́лся]? Panfyorov loves these words just as Gladkov loves сбы́чился [упря́мился]. Why should трясогу́зка (wagtail) be replaced by трясу́ха?...Panfyorov writes the word про́клят (damned) as he hears it: про́клит...The over-use of provincialisms and dialect phrases interferes as much with clarity of expression as does the forcing of foreign words into Russian phrases. There is no point in writing конденса́ция when we have a perfectly good word of our own—сгуще́ние.

Naturally Soviet literature is far from following the above advice in a blind, mechanical way. Its true value is not as a specific rule but as a guiding principle. It would be impossible from this point of view to reach, for instance, a proper appraisal of Mayakovsky's poetry, which cannot be expressed in any language but his own, deeply rooted as it is in the colourful, agitated and familiar vernacular with its somewhat offhand and picturesque roughness. The systematic use of a certain number of dialectisms is an integral feature of Sholokhov's style, e.g. ажник 'even', гута́рить 'speak', зара́з 'at once', тро́шки 'a little', etc. But in so far as the language of literature is based upon the same foundations as the written language used for general purposes, it still continues to develop along the well-tried path of blending colloquial and literary language into a single whole. It is as much a case of the vernacular being raised to literary status, as it is of the literary language becoming the inalienable heritage of Russian everyday life. There is no need to demonstrate that it is this vital and durable link with the traditions of the 'classical' period of its development which has given the contemporary Russian literary language the function of being not only the common language of the Russian people, but also the common official language of the whole commonwealth of peoples which make up the USSR. In this respect also the Russian language continues, in new and more favourable conditions, to play the role which it has gradually assumed as the second (and not infrequently even the first) language of the intelligentsia of the various non-Russian nationalities inhabiting Russia.

FURTHER READING

Unfortunately, relatively few works exist in English on the history of Russian. Some of these, and a few of the most useful works in other languages, are listed below.

General

Matthews, W. K. *Russian Historical Grammar*. London, 1960. [A more technical work than Vinokur.]

Matthews, W. K. *The Structure and Development of Russian*. London, 1953. [Covers ground similar to that of Vinokur, but in a more condensed and technical way.]

Entwistle, W. J. and Morison, W. A. *Russian and the Slavonic Languages*. London, 1949. [The presentation and style make this a difficult book to read. Mostly restricted to phonology and morphology and somewhat out-of-date.]

Among the most useful works in Russian are:

Borkovsky, V. I. and Kuznetsov, P. S. *Историческая грамматика русского языка*. Moscow, 1963.

Bulakhovsky, L. A. *Исторический комментарий к русскому литературному языку*. Various editions 1936 onwards.

Levin, V. D. *Краткий очерк истории русского литературного языка*. Moscow, 1964.

Vinogradov, V. V. *Русский язык. Грамматическое учение о слове*. Moscow, 1947.

Texts

Sources of specific texts are given in detail in some of the general works listed above. Here only the most useful collections are mentioned.

Obnorsky, S. P. and Barkhudarov, S. G. *Хрестоматия по истории русского языка*, ч. *1*. Moscow, 1952. [The most favoured anthology from the linguistic point of view.]

Gudzy, N. K. *Хрестоматия по древней русской литературе*. Moscow, various editions. [A good selection of literary texts up to the 17th century.]

139

Further reading

Kokorev, A. V. *Хрестоматия по русской литературе XVIII века.* Moscow, various editions.

Stender-Petersen, A. and Congrat-Butlar, S. *Anthology of Old Russian Literature.* New York, 1954. [Particularly useful for its notes and glossary.]

The Slavonic Languages

De Bray, R. G. A. *A Guide to the Slavonic Languages.* London, 1951 and 1969. [An encyclopaedic work describing the phonology and morphology of all the Slavonic languages, including Old Church Slavonic, mainly in tabular form.]

Kondrashov, N. A. *Славянские языки.* Moscow, 1956. [A brief but systematic treatment useful to students.]

Dialects

Matthews, W. K. 'Modern Russian Dialects', *Transactions of the Philological Society*, 1950, pp. 112–48.

Vocabulary and Etymology

The standard etymological dictionary is:

Vasmer, M. *Russisches etymologisches Wörterbuch.* 3 vols. Heidelberg, 1953–8. [Also published in a Soviet edition with some omissions.]

Shansky, N. M. and others. *Краткий этимологический словарь русского языка.* Moscow, 1961. [A handy one-volume work which is not however entirely reliable.]

Chernykh, P. Ya. *Очерк русской исторической лексикологии.* Moscow, 1956. [Deals with the vocabulary up to the 17th century.]

Huttl Worth, G. *Foreign Words in Russian. A Historical Sketch, 1550–1800.* Berkeley, Cal., 1963.

Gardiner, S. C. *German Loanwords in Russian 1550–1690.* (Publications of the Philological Society, xxi.) Oxford, 1965.

The history of Russian personal names is treated in a concise and interesting manner in:

Chichagov, V. K. *Из истории русских имен, отчеств и фамилий.* Moscow, 1959.

Further reading

Palaeography and alphabet

Cherepnin, A. V. *Русская палеография*. Moscow, 1956. [A full description, with many illustrations, of the scripts used in Russia up to the early 19th century.]

Shitsgal, A. *Русский гражданский шрифт 1708–1958*. Moscow, 1959. [An illustrated history of the modern printed alphabet.]

Various periods

Unbegaun, B. O. *La langue russe au XVIe siècle. I. La flexion des noms*. Paris, 1935.

Vinogradov, V. V. *The History of the Russian Literary Language from the 17th Century to the 19th*. Madison, Wis., 1969. [A 'condensed adaptation' of his *Очерки по истории русского литературного языка XVII–XIX веков*. Moscow, 1938.]

Chukovsky, K. I. *Живой как жизнь*. Moscow, 1963. [An interesting popular discussion of contemporary Russian, particularly concerned with modern developments which the author considers undesirable.]

Unbegaun, B. O. 'Colloquial and Literary Russian', *Oxford Slavonic Papers*, *1*, 1950, pp. 26–36.

Ward, D. *The Russian Language Today. System and Anomaly*. London, 1965. [Mainly a description of the contemporary language, but historical material is adduced where necessary, and the possible path of further development of Russian in the future is suggested.]

Bibliographies

Unbegaun, B. O. and Simmons, J. S. G. *A Bibliographical Guide to the Russian Language*. Oxford, 1953.

Less comprehensive, but sometimes more up-to-date bibliographies appear in the books by W. K. Matthews listed above, and selective classified lists with useful annotations in:

Horecky, P. L. *Basic Russian Publications. An annotated Bibliography on Russia and the Soviet Union*. Chicago, 1962, pp. 182–6. [Lists works in the Cyrillic alphabet.]

Horecky, P. L. *Russia and the Soviet Union. A Bibliographical Guide to Western Language Publications*. Chicago, 1965, pp. 269–76.

Further reading

Two works still in preparation when the present edition went to press, which will provide more extensive and up-to-date information, are volume IV of *Guide to Russian Reference Books* (Hoover Institute Bibliographical Series) edited by Karol Maichel, and volume II of *A Selected Bibliography of Slavic Linguistics* by E. Stankiewicz and D. S. Worth.

INDEX

adjectives 6, 12, 14, 47–8, 67; comparative, 13
akanie 13–15, 18–19, 40, 70, 87*n*, 103, 118
Aleksey Mikhaylovich, Tsar 40, 83, 93
alphabet:
    Cyrillic 23, 25–8, 141
    Glagolitic 25–7
    reform of 86, 88, 132
    see also orthography, script
aorist *see* verb
archaisms 117
Archangel *see* Evangeliary
Armoury Museum, Moscow 30
Arzamas Society 119
Avvakum, Archpriest 38, 94–6

Baltic languages 3, 6, 40
Batyushkov, K. N. 115–16, 121
Belorussian 1, 8–9, 15, 18, 20, 41, 68, 70, 87
Bible 90
birch-bark documents 37
Bitaubé, P. J. 104
Boborykin, P. D. 114
Bolotov, A. T. 106, 111
'bookish' *see* styles
Boris and Gleb, Legend of 37, 45, 76
borrowings *see* vocabulary
Bukharin, N. 136
Bulgarian 1, 6, 8, 22–4, 26–8, 35–6, 48, 52, 61, 71, 76–7; *see also* South Slavonic influence
Byzantium 21–2, 24, 27, 34, 35, 53, 58*n*, 67

calques 110, 114, 133
cases:
    accusative 13
    dative 13, 68–9
    dative absolute 67, 93
    genitive in -y 46–7
    genitive-accusative 6, 46
    genitive with negation 7
    genitive plural 47

instrumental 7, 13, 93
    nominative 102
    nominative absolute 67
    vocative 6, 15, 19, 45–6, 69, 128
chancellery *see* styles
Chasoslov 89
Chekhov, A. P. 128–9
Chet'i-minei see *Minei*
chokanie 12
Christianity, role of 21–2, 27
Chronicles 16, 34, 50, 58, 62–3
    George Hamartolos 38
    Hypatian 38, 62
    Königsberg 38, 50
    Laurentian 36–7, 48, 58, 62
    Novgorod 37, 64
    Primary 34, 37, 59, 65–7
    Radziwill 38, 50
Chulkov, M. D. 110
Church *see* Christianity
Church Slavonic *see* Slavonic, Old Church
Codex Marianus 26
Codex Supraslensis 26
Codex Zographensis 25, 26
Common Slavonic 1, 3
conjugation *see* verb
consonants:
    clusters 43, 76–7
    devoiced 87
    hush-sibilants 44
    mutations 5, 8, 15
    velar 5, 12, 14–15, 19, 43, 70, 103, 118, 125, 128
Constantine *see* Cyril
Constantinople 70
contractions 135
Coptic 26
Cyril 22–4, 26–8, 35
Cyrillic alphabet *see* alphabet
Czech 1, 8

Daniil, the Exile 59, 61–2, 65
Decembrists 117–18
declensions 6, 45–8, 53*n*, 102, 106, 117

Index

dialects 10–20, 39–40, 82, 127–8, 137, 140
  eastern 16, 18
  northern 10–13, 19, 40–1
  middle 14–15, 18–19
  Moscow 19, 38, 82
  Novgorod 36
  Pskov 14, 39–40, 57, 82
  Smolensk 37, 40
  southern 13–14, 19
direct/indirect speech 66–7
Dmitriev, I. I. 119–21
Dobrilov's Gospels see Gospels
documents 32, 36–7, 55–7, 77–80, 87–8
Dolgorukaya, Natal'ya 88–9
Domostroi 38, 80–1
Dostoyevsky, F. M. 127, 129–30, 131
doublets, lexical 61–4, 76–7, 94
Dovmont, Prince 57
dual number 6, 45, 69, 96

ě *see* vowels
East Slavonic 8–9, 15–19, 27, 29, 35, 41, 68
ecclesiastical *see* styles
education, language of 101
Evangeliary 23, 35; Archangel 29, 35

Feodosiy, Life of 37
Florinsky, Kirill 92
folklore 51, 58, 124
Fonvizin, D. I. 104, 109, 111–12, 121, 124
French 98, 108, 110–14, 119
futurism 131
Fyodorov, Ivan 39

Galicia 39
gender 14
genres 99, 102–3, 106, 118
German 1, 22, 64, 133
gerund *see* verb
Gistoriya o... Vasilii Koriotskom 92–3, 97
Gladkov, F. V. 137
Glagolitic *see* alphabet
Gleb, Prince 30; *Legend of Boris and Gleb see* Boris
Gogol', N. V. 67, 127, 129–30, 133

Gor'ky, A. M. 129, 137
Gospels:
  Archangel 29
  Dobrilov 36
  Galician 36
  Mstislav 36
  Ostromir 25, 26, 34–5, 43
gramoty see documents
'Great Russian' 20
Grech, N. I. 132
Greek 21–4, 26, 35–6, 43, 67, 102, 109, 133
Griboyedov, A. S. 108, 111, 132–3
Grigoriy, Deacon 34–5
Grot, Ya. K. 132

hard sign *see* vowels, reduced
Hebrew 26
Hegel, F. 133–4
Hermitage, the (Leningrad) 30
Herzen, A. I. 134
homonyms 64–5
Hypatian *see* Chronicles
hypotaxis 65

Igor, Prince *see Slovo*
Ilarion, Metropolitan 38, 53–4, 61
Indo-European languages 1–4, 6–7
inscriptions 30–1
intelligentsia 109
Istoriya o Aleksandre 93–4
Iuar, St 73–4
Ivan Kalita 37
Ivan IV, the Terrible 38, 40, 73, 75
Izborniki Svyatoslava see Svyatoslav
Izmaylov, A. E. 120
izvitie sloves 53–5, 71–3, 90–1

Josephus 62

Kantemir, A. D. 105
Kapnist, V. V. 103
Karamzin, N. M. 44–5, 50, 98–9, 107–8, 112–15, 117–21, 125, 132
Katyryov-Rostovsky, I. M., Prince 74–7
Kheraskov, M. M. 100, 103
Kiev 16, 18, 19, 35
Kievan Rus' *see* Rus'
Kirill, Bishop of Turov 38, 54, 61, 65, 76
Klyuchevsky, V. O. 109

Index

Königsberg *see* Chronicles
Kotoshikhin 38, 83–4
Krylov, I. A. 120–1, 124
Kulikovo, Battle of 38
Kurbsky, Prince Andrey 38, 75, 80
Kyukhelbeker, V. K. 117, 119

Laurentian *see* Chronicles
Law Code of 1649 38–9, 80
learned *see* styles
Lenin, V. I. 136–7
Leskov, N. S. 129
Levshin, V. A. 100
literacy 86–7, 89
'literary language' 20, 21, 24, 28, 52, 57, 83, 92, 99, 126, 138
literature, role of 89, 92, 96–107, 126–31
Lithuanian 3–5, 8
loan translations *see* calques
Lomonosov, M. V. 21–2, 24, 89–90, 97, 99, 101–3, 110, 112, 118–19
Ludolf, Wilhelm 88
Lukin, V. I. 112

Makariy, Metropolitan 73
manuscripts 25–6, 30–2, 34, 37–9
Matinsky, M. A. 106
Mayakovsky, V. V. 131, 137
Maykov, V. I. 103
Mazon, A. 34*n*
Meillet, A. 21
Menaea see *Minei*
meshchanstvo 129
Methodius 22–4, 26, 28, 35
Michael III, Emperor 22–3
Minei 35–6, 73–4, 89
Miscellany, Uspensky Cathedral 37; *Svyatoslav's Miscellanies see* Svyatoslav
Mojmir 22
Moravia 22–5, 27–8
Moscow 19, 37, 40, 70–1, 77, 81, 87
Mstislav Davidovich, Prince 56
Mstislav, Grand Prince 36
Mstislav's Gospel *see* Gospels
Muscovy 68–9, 70–1, 82, 87
Musin-Pushkin, A. I., Count 34*n*, 39

Narezhny, V. T. 121
narodnost' 94, 120, 124, 126
nasal vowels *see* vowels, nasal

Nekrasov, N. A. 133
neologisms 47, 83, 92–3, 109–10, 114, 119*n*, 132–5
Nestor 38*n*
Nikitin, Afanasiy 38
Nikol'sky, N. K. 27
Nikon, Patriarch 90
Novgorod 37
Novgorod chronicles *see* Chronicles
Novgorod Minei see *Minei*

Obnorsky, S. P. 55
Odoyevsky, N. I., Prince 79
okanie 10, 15, 19, 40, 70, 125
Old Church Slavonic *see* Slavonic, Old Church
Old Russian literature 34
Oleg, Prince 34, 50–1, 62
orthography 23, 26–8, 40, 43–5, 69–71, 82, 87*n*, 88–9, 131–2
Ostromir *see* Gospels
Ostrovsky, A. N. 129

palatalization 5, 8–9, 15, 39, 42–4, 68
Panfyorov, F. I. 137
parataxis 65
participles *see* verb
particle -то, -от 13, 106
Perevoshchikov, D. M. 134
perfect tense *see* verb
Peter I 30, 47, 70, 85–7, 92, 94, 101, 110, 118
petitions 78–9
Petrov, V. P. 103
phonology 4–6, 8–9, 10–15, 28, 39, 41–5, 69–70, 76, 103
Pisarev, D. I. 135
pleophony 8, 29, 61–4, 76
pluperfect *see* verb
plural of nouns 15, 45
poetic diction 104–5
Polikarpov, F. 85–6, 90
Polish 1, 5, 8, 9, 16, 18, 22, 40
polnoglasie see pleophony
Polotsky Simeon 87*n*
Pososhkov, I. T. 70
postpositive article *see* particle -то, -от
Potebnya, A. A. 65
Pouchenie Vladimira Monomakha see Vladimir Monomakh
Povest' vremennykh let see Chronicles

Index

prikazy see styles, chancellery
Primary Chronicle see Chronicles
printed books 38–9
Prokopovich, Feofan 91
pronouns 12, 14
pronunciation see phonology
prostonarodnost' 102, 106, 108, 120, 122–3, 128, 131, 136
Prussian, Old 40
Psalter 58, 89
Pskov dialect see dialects
Pushkin, A. S. 24, 47, 50, 106, 109–10, 114, 117–19, 121–6, 132–3

Radishchev, A. N. 101
rhetoric see *izvitie sloves*
Rostislav 22–3
Rus' 16, 19, 20*n*, 27, 31, 34*n*, 58, 68–9
'Russian language' 10, 18–20, 81–3, 107, 121
Russkaya Pravda 37, 55–7
Ryleyev, K. F. 117

Salonika 2, 22
Saltykov-Shchedrin, M. E. 129
satem languages 4
Sbornik see *Miscellany*
script 141
    cursive 32–3
    half-uncial 32–3
    uncial 25, 26, 32
    see also alphabet
Selishchev, A. M. 40
Sentimentalism 108, 112
Serbo-Croatian 1, 8, 24, 26, 28
Shakhmatov, A. A. 16, 18–19
Sheremetev, F. I. 78–9
Shishkov, A. S. 118–19, 120, 124–5
Sholokhov, M. A. 137
Simeon, Tsar 23, 35
Slavonic, Old Church 1, 21–4, 27–9, 34–5, 39, 41, 43, 49*n*, 52, 55, 61–5, 69, 71, 76–7, 82, 86–7, 90–2, 94, 96–7, 99, 101, 110, 118–19
Slavonic languages 1, 4–9, 140; see also Common Slavonic, East Slavonic, South Slavonic
Slavonic tribes 16–20
'Slavonicisms' 62–4, 69, 70, 76, 79, 93–4, 96, 101–3, 105, 116–17
Slovo o polku Igoreve 34, 38–9, 58, 62, 65

Slovo o zakone i blagodati see Ilarion
Smotritsky, Meletiy 87, 89, 101
Sobolevsky, A. I. 36, 39
soft sign see vowels, reduced
South Slavonic influence 32, 43, 61–4, 70–3, 77
Soviet period 135–8
Stefan Permskiy 71–2
Stoglav 38
stress 10, 13–14, 42, 70, 90
styles 52, 80–1
    bookish 52, 68–9, 76, 94, 109, 121
    business 52, 55–7, 77–80, 83–4, 86
    chancellery 77–82, 86
    ecclesiastical 52–5, 76, 86, 94
    high 86, 90, 99, 102–4, 107
    learned 52–5, 69, 76, 85
    literary 52, 57–62
    low 99, 100, 102, 106–7
    middle 89, 99–102, 104, 107–9, 114
Sumarokov, A. P. 100, 103, 105, 111
Svyatopolk, Prince, of Moravia 23
Svyatoslav, Prince, of Kiev, *Miscellanies* 35
syllables 4–6, 8, 42–3
synonyms, Russian and Church Slavonic see doublets, lexical
syntax 65–7, 76, 80, 101

Tallemant, P. 97
Tatars 15, 18, 37*n*, 38
Timofeyev, Ivan 73
Tmutorokan' stone 30
Tolstoy, L. N. 127–8
translations, role of 22–4, 83, 85–6, 101, 104, 109
Trediakovsky, V. K. 88–9, 97–9, 102, 108, 110, 136
tsokanie 12, 36
Turgenev, I. S. 128, 130
Turks 70

Ukraine 87
Ukrainian 1, 9, 15, 18–20, 36, 41, 68, 70, 87
Ulozhenie see Law Code
uncial see script
Upyr' Likhoy 27

Varenius 85–6
Varlaam 36
Vasiliy III, Grand Prince 77–8

Index

Vaugelas, C. F. de 98
Vedomosti 47, 85
verb:
  aorist 48, 49, 69, 73, 93, 96
  aspect 7, 49n
  gerund 13, 50
  imperfect 48, 69, 73
  participles 49, 50, 67, 103, 118
  past in *l* 9, 13, 40, 49
  perfect 48
  pluperfect 49
  present 13–14, 103
  stems 103, 106
  'to be' 7
vernacular 41, 52, 55, 68, 73, 76,
  79–80, 82, 90, 92, 97, 102, 121
Vladimir Davydovich, Prince 30
Vladimir Monomakh 58–9, 61, 63–6
vocabulary 7, 13, 14, 23, 27, 61–5, 76,
  109, 132–7, 140
vocative *see* cases
Volhynia 39
Vostokov, A. Kh. 35, 132
vowels:
  back 4

ĕ 42, 44–5, 69–70, 103, 118
fleeting 42
front 4
nasal 8–9, 28, 43
'reduced' 28, 42–3, 71
yat' 9, 12, 41–2, 90, 103
Vsyakaya Vsyachina 100
vulgarisms *see prostonarodnost'*
Vyazemsky, P. A. 123

Western Slavonic 19, 23
word-formation 72–3, 132–5

yakanie 14
Yaroslav, the Wise 37n, 45, 56
Yavorsky, Stefan 87n, 90
yat' *see* vowels
Yepifaniy, the Wise 71–2
yers *see* vowels, 'reduced'
yus, big and *small* 28, 43, 71

Zadonshchina 38
Zagoskin, M. N. 117
Zhukovsky, V. A. 115–18, 121
Zimin, A. A. 34n